D0927579

FORCE
MAGNIFIER

the cultural impacts of artificial intelligence

other **Wildside Press** books by Michael Betancourt

Two Women and a Nightengale

Artemis: A Tragedy of Collage

Those Hidden Obstructions

Re–Viewing Miami

Structuring Time:
notes on making movies

Harmonia:
Glitch, Movies and Visual Music

The History of Motion Graphics:
from avant–garde to industry in the United States

A Short Guide to Writing About Motion Graphics

Visual Music Instrument Patents

Mary Hallock–Greenewalt: The Complete Patents

Thomas Wilfred's Lumia

A. Wallace Rimington's Colour–Music

FORCE MAGNIFIER

the cultural impacts of artificial intelligence

MICHAEL BETANCOURT

WILDSIDE PRESS

Published by Wildside Press, LLC.
www.wildsidepress.com

Copyright © 2020 Michael Betancourt, all rights reserved

Cover artwork:
instaglitch_41476766_2209971759249345_425094765525400455_n.jpg
copyright © 2018 Michael Betancourt / Artists Rights Society (ARS)

Aspects of this analysis are drawn from *The Critique of Digital Capitalism: An Analysis of the Political Economy of Digital Culture and Technology*, Punctum Books, 2016.

Other parts of this book were adapted from previous publications produced in earlier stages of this analysis:

"Article: a107, Disruptive Technology: The Avant–Gardness of Avant–Garde Art" *CTheory*, 2002.

"Theory Beyond the Codes: 058, The Demands of Agnotology::Surveillance" *CTheory*, 2014.

"Theorizing 21c: 21C012, The Limits of Utility," *CTheory*, 2015.

"Theorizing 21c: 21C031, The Paradox of Agency," *CTheory*, 2016.

Ideologies of the Real in Title Sequences, Motion Graphics and Cinema (New York: Routledge, 2019).

Additional materials concerning automation, return on investment, and the issues of social media are adapted from material posed on *Cinegraphic.net*.

ISBN 9781479448197 PERFECT
ISBN 9781479448203 CASEBOUND

This is a copyrighted work protected by intellectual property laws in the United States and other countries. The digitizing, scanning, uploading, or distribution of this book via the Internet or via any other means without the permission of the publisher is illegal and punishable by law. Please purchase only authorized electronic editions of this book, and do not encourage, enable, or participate in book piracy. Your support of author's rights is appreciated.

for Leah

CONTENTS

FIGURES

ACKNOWLEDGEMENTS

No analysis can ever fully recognize the influences and impacts that shaped its development. In preparing this discussion of autonomous agency, what became apparent are the ways that my thinking about judgments and social processes have been shaped over many years through discussions and contacts with a diverse collection of individuals too numerous to readily identify. Returning to foundational texts always involves a revisiting of ones sources and early influences; any return to origins is never an easy or comfortable task. Parts of this present analysis are derived from discussions with my colleagues Greg Johnson and John Collette who provided useful insights and comments in my discussions with them while this analysis was in progress.

I must also acknowledge the instrumental role the *Aspen Institute–Germany* played in my writing of this critique since it is a direct result of their invitation to speak at the *Aspen–Berlin AI Conference 2020, Humanity Enabled: AI & the Great Economic Awakening,* on March 25 and 26. Without their prompt, this project would not exist. What began as my address for this conference has grown in to the present analysis, an expansion of scope and depth that has extended my earlier observations on digital capitalism into a critique of the Enlightenment ideologies that have been reified in both capitalist production and the social.

Frontis: The robot Marius (Gilbert Ritchie) along with two manual
labor robots on stage with Harry Domin (Basil Rathbone) and
Helena Glory (Frances Carson) in Act 1 of a performance of Karel
Čapek's play *Rossumovi Univerzální Roboti* (*Rossum's Universal
Robots*) at St. Martin's Theatre, London, England, 1923.

PREFACE

Sometimes books "write themselves"—for a discussion of artificial intelligence (AI), this seemed appropriate. What began as a presentation for the third annual conference on AI hosted by the *Aspen Institute–Germany* in March 2020 about the cultural impacts related to both automation and autonomous agency rapidly took shape as a book because this topic could not be fully addressed to my satisfaction in the relatively brief form of a lecture. My investigation of artificial intelligence starts with an apparently simple question that rapidly opens onto an ideological superstructure derived from the Enlightenment, that period that gave birth to the industrial revolution, and which continues to dictate the order of digital capitalism: *What exactly does AI automate?* This question has posed significant difficulties in the past, problematizing analysis of its impacts.[1] The solution adopted in this study relies on Immanuel Kant's distinction between determinative judgment and reflective judgment to identify the scope of intelligent actions being automated and their social, cultural, and political significance for an emergent 'society of leisure.'

My analysis of these impacts is preliminary, suggesting avenues and directions of exploration that identify transitional barriers to a post-labor economy. But this is not a book of economics nor a technical analysis of AI—instead it considers their emergent interactions and properties.[2] The conflicts it describes are not dialectical oppositions, but fluid convergences of social and cultural beliefs and ideologies; nevertheless there are shared foundations which allow a degree of generalization. The exemplars chosen to illustrate this argument are precise instances of specific applications of AI, chosen because of their utility for this singular argument that emerged directly from my own need to elaborate on how the complex underpinnings of this fundamental shift suggests a cultural redefinition of labor and value. This analysis expands upon my earlier discussions in *The Critique of Digital Capitalism* and *The Digital Agent versus Human Agency*. Where the analysis in the former was concerned with the structural changes to the political economy wrought by digital technology, the latter analysis concerned how digital capitalism acts to capture human agency and prevent dissent; AI is an implicit element of both discussions. The analysis in *Force Magnifier* revisits key concepts proposed in these earlier studies as expressions of an Enlightenment idealization of rational thought that becomes a cultural driver for the divergent potentials of artificial intelligence and machine learning as well as the invention of autonomous agency. This discursive analysis addresses how the automation of human agency interacts with my earlier concepts— especially the aura of the digital, the scarcity of capital, and the limits of utility—as well as the proposition that in abandoning its historical commodity basis, currency becomes a title to initiate future production.

Acknowledging the structural changes apparent in this 'great decoupling' of wealth from gains in employment and the productive activity of labor requires a recognition that machine learning has created a radical exodus from the predictable dislocations and transformations known from earlier mechanical automation. For this analysis, there is no difference between weak AI that addresses specialized tasks and the smarter, strong AI that handles more complex problems: the cultural impacts originating with AI are constant. The displacement of human labor does not distinguish between weak or strong since it is the same human agency being replaced in either type. This impact becomes coherent as an expansion of the priorities formerly only granted to the top of the societal hierarchy—the proposition of the 'society of leisure' arises in the elimination of human labor from production, thus a post-labor economy. This potentially democratic expansion is not a utopian fantasy, but a critical struggle to understand the nature of these changes, and the structural drivers/impediments that become cultural barriers to stability. Consequently, this argument has a nodal form, recrossing its own paths in an attempt to define and demarcate the interaction–convergence emanating from within digital capitalism and aspects of social and cultural order that it makes appear to be natural.

However, what defines the post-labor economy is not the complete elimination of human labor from production, but the removal of human agency from the production of value. This shift is apparent in how the invention of AI promises structural unemployment for any field whose primary labor is rote performance or manipulation of a fixed set of rules, no matter how complex and specialized.[3] This technological revolution is different from earlier automation: the speed and nature of this replacement diverges from how new technology has historically shifted the role for human labor to other roles in production, but maintained human labor as the foundation of value. The post-labor economy quickly replaces this basis in human agency, replacing both the labor and the value production with a machine: consider how the elimination of human labor for processes such as printing a page of text took centuries to complete—what in Gutenberg's time required substantial human labor is now autonomously performed by the computer printer without human oversight. This capacity to replace human labor with automation is emerging at a much faster rate of technical development and deployment; instead of centuries, it takes place over months or years.[4] The change this shift produces for the nature of value marks the shift to post-labor. The ideology of disruption, evident in the application of digital technology (*Facebook's* "move fast and break things") and understood as an unquestionably positive factor in industry, has enabled this speed of emergence to enter into conflict with the established structure of capitalism, bringing its impacts on wealth and value to attention as the 'great decoupling.' This new capacity to automate what had formerly been exclusively the domain of human intellectual activity suggests a fundamental redefinition of all human labor, a change that directly undermines the existing social order dependent on these fixed relationships and the societal hierarchy capitalism produced.

How the embrace of AI disrupts value depends on what it replaces: the types of agency associated with labor rather than management, factors identified by different types of productive action that, in turn, define class distinctions and limit mobility, but are socially revealed through differentials of wealth. These anthropological factors around the mass of human labor working in the factory defines the ways that wealth, equality, and leisure function—and they also inform the different appraisals of social position derived from both un/employment and apparent wealth in a system of cultural value expressed financially that economist Joseph Schumpeter observed in capitalist societies:

> There is an element of truth in the brutal slogan of the
> typical bourgeois which many worthy men find so
> irritating, viz., that those who cannot climb by these ladders
> [of success] are not worth troubling about.[5]

His statement expresses a high social dominance orientation: an understanding of social standing as a fixed distribution within the societal hierarchy, recognizable as objectification and the dismissal of concern for anyone who is at lower tier, for example, in their denigration as being lazy, dirty, stupid, and uneducated. Economic status depends on employment, and its accompanying asymmetries and inequality becomes the inevitable result/proof of lower intelligence and moral decrepitude. It reveals the ideological influence of reformation theology focused on work defined by the "Protestant Work Ethic" that developed in the nineteenth century as a justification for the wealth, power, and privilege of the industrial bourgeoisie—a belief that "disciplined pursuit of individual self-interest was a moral imperative; prosperity was dependent on virtue."[6] The American myth of the "self-made man" claims that to be poor or unsuccessful economically was a demonstration of being immoral, intellectually inferior, and 'hated by God'—a position reinforced by the lesser education and diminished prospects for the inchoate mass of labor employed in the factory. Economic success was conceived in this ideology as a pure proof of self-actualized will, moral superiority, and divine blessing—it transforms the Feudal "divine right" for a mercantile society, and authorizes the concentration of corporate power that is so evident in the international scope of digital capitalism. This legitimation of historical capitalist hierarchy masks the managerial labor whose decisions impact all social, cultural, political, and economic activity with a disavowal of personal responsibility that matches the aura of the digital's refusal to consider the physical costs, material limits, and environmental impacts in capitalist production. The post-labor economy emerges form the convergence of this ideological superstructure with the technological capacity to eliminate human agency from production—thus from value generation—allowing the aura of the digital to instrumentalize the fantasy of value generation without labor. This ideology of "autonomous achievement" justifies the use of AI to eliminate the role of this socially insignificant mass of human labor whose judgments had little importance, but whose actions created value. It affirms the belief that only the highest levels of management, the CEO and board of directors—those individuals who are members of the economically privileged upper classes and whose views on "success" Schumpeter relays—matter for value production. The 'society of leisure' has always existed for this dominant minority; AI suggests its potential expansion to a much larger section of human society.

The cultural myths that haunt autonomous systems—whether the homunculus or golem of the past, or the more recent terrors of a "robot apocalypse" that informs even Karel Čapek's play *Rossumovi Univerzální Roboti* (*Rossum's Universal Robots*, 1921)—do little to address the issues faced by the post-labor economy and the proposal of the 'society of leisure.' Recognizing the social impacts of AI begins identifying the type of agency being automated, since not all forms of human agency have the same cultural importance, and not all forms of 'intelligence' are useful in production, nor act to displace human agency. What is of general social concern are those forms of automated agency (AI) that eliminate the costs of living labor and replace them with an unpaid machine; this discussion only considers issues connected to those applications of weak and strong AI.

Acknowledging that there are distinct varieties of human agency reveals internal differences between managerial decisions (reflective judgments) and the agency used by labor (determinative judgments). Whose agency is being automated is what matters. The different cultural importance given to these categories of agency shapes the types of labor being automated, as well as accounts for the structural drive to replace human labor in more than simply economic terms. The underlying problem this revolutionary technology raises for human society is *will it increase wealth without diminishing the misery of poverty?* This issue, the fair and equitable distribution of commodities, concerns the way that capitalism has solved the distribution problem through the payment of wages that human labor then recycles to purchase the results of their labor. In historical capitalism it was possible to fold these issues of production and distribution into the same theoretical construct due to the cycle of wages::profits.[7] The capacity to eliminate human labor decouples these formerly linked aspects of commodity distribution, creating a structural contradiction with economic, political, and cultural impacts—the 'great decoupling.' Automation and AI pose a potential for cascading breakdowns in the cultural order of capitalism by abolishing the need for entire categories of human labor without necessarily creating equivalent new labor for those workers.[8] These changes are unlike earlier displacements of low-skilled labor by machines that created demand for new, highly skilled professional expertise—these highly skilled positions are now being replaced, a change that may create structural unemployment for workers in professional fields such as law, medicine, and education. Unlike the automation of manufacturing, AI does not necessarily result in a zero-sum outcome where the displaced labor simply moves into a new type of employment.[9] These breaches in the historical norms of technological unemployment are the 'great decoupling' developing with the shift to digital automation and AI.

Defining the Post-Labor Economy

The proposal of human labor becoming obsolete is neither new nor aberrant when considering industrialization. The contemporary uncertainty about what these deviations from the historical *status quo* of capitalism will actually produce in the post-labor economy is an indicator that we are living though a transitional period that makes the need for critical analysis acute. The total elimination of human labor has long stood as a distant, hypothetical goal, long considered a ridiculous fringe proposal for economics. But reducing human labor was an explicit goal for the economics of John Maynard Keynes in the 1930s; it has returned as a concern of heterodox economic theories as well as in mainstream discourse with the contemporary invention of AI and its capacity to replace human labor with an autonomous device. However, what defines the 'post-labor economy' is not an end to all human labor, but the decentering of human labor from the production of value in a dismissal and idling of human activity that imposes a basic redefinition of value away from the Enlightenment's reification of human agency as a commodity: 'post-labor' does not mean humans are no longer working, but that human agency is no longer the foundation of value. This change in role comes without necessarily concluding the heritage of capitalism in the political, cultural, and social organization of society. The problems of such a society are not well-theorized, but have been an enduring subject of the utopian and dystopian fantasies of science-fiction. With the advent AI a post-labor economy is no longer a fantasy, even though the suggestion of an immanent "Fully Automated Luxury Communism"[10] remains a fantasy created by the aura of the digital's erasure of physicality and material limits from consciousness.

The transition to the 'society of leisure' implied by the post-labor economy is blocked by established social, cultural, political, religious and even economic ideologies. The change it creates for value production confronts revenant impedimenta that arose in response to ground conditions that have changed: they are derived from the priorities of the infopoor society that developed archival, religious and social beliefs in response to its high infant mortality rate, short life expectancy, and an agrarian organization around subsistence where commodities were difficult to produce, labor-intensive, expensive—factors that do not describe the general availability and accumulation under digital capitalism, nor even under the earlier industrial capitalism: it makes the vast human population that reflects both the discovery of antibiotics and improvements in medical care as well as the financial need for a large body of human labor to work in the factories into complementary, self-reinforcing developments. While a reduction in infant mortality is a positive value, when the birth rate does not adjust to reflect that change, major problems with the food supply are only a few generations away from manifesting as a product of over population. This consequence illustrates the ways that technological change turns successful historical adaptive behaviors into impedimenta and emergent challenges.

These foundations inherited from the infopoor society translate directly into the technology of digital automation. This development of post-labor via AI systems is the logical outcome of the Enlightenment's rationalist, empirical ideology becoming the instrumentality of technology: Modernist priorities reified in the digital technologies of automation and autonomous agency demands adherence to an absolute and unchanging "truth" that is determined in advance. Thus the apparatus being limited to operating only within a predetermined range matches the cultural demands imposed upon it; a restriction that renders its unintelligent replacement of human labor an expression of the class distinctions inherited from these earlier social orders. These social hierarchies/differences inform sociologist Thorstein Veblen's critique of productive action–as–agency that recalls the discussion of human agency and rational judgment by the Enlightenment philosopher Immanuel Kant:

> As a matter of selective necessity, man is an agent. He is, in his own apprehension, a center of the unfolding impulsive activity—"teleological" activity. His is an agent seeking in every act the accomplishment of some concrete, objective, impersonal end. By force of his being such an agent he is possessed of a taste for effective work, and a distaste for futile effort.[11]

The "teleological" impulse employs self-conscious motivation (agency) as the material substance of human productivity. Agency in this analysis is not the act of following an established rule, as in a machine, but an independent decision guided by human desire that sets the on-demand production of digital capitalism in motion. This motivation is the apotheosis of the distinction between human agency and the autonomous agency of AI. The machine is merely an apparatus that meets and responds to the true reason for its operation: human desires. This view of agency in the sociological analysis by Veblen is an Enlightenment construct that returns to the distinctions between reflective and determinative judgments Kant proposed at the beginning of the industrial revolution.[12] Veblen assumes this commodification of agency as the inherent and necessary organization of social relations— their role as expressions of social distinction—giving it an eternal character as the central use for commodities once they are separated from the necessity of sustaining life; however, what is immanent in the 'society of leisure' is not a utopia of abundance, freedom, and equality that breaks with how historical capitalism valorized human agency—that is a fantasy prompted by the aura of the digital—but an expansion of the social class that is denied a role in production. The historical leisure classes were culturally blocked from productive labor; this group is what expands with the post-labor economy.

The social, cultural and political consequences of AI replacing human labor depends upon what the continued role of human agency will be, and how it will function in relation to the commodities created by this inhuman labor and production by autonomous machines; at the same time, the complementary and direct issues of the societal hierarchy that constrain how to equitably distribute production become the most important unknown in this change. Replacing wages with some form of largesse, either a dividend, a stipend, or other form of unearned salary such as 'universal basic income' is an approach that addresses the issue of distribution through the 'solution' of maintaining the existing cycle of wages::profits; however, the changes needed are more than just a matter of palliatives such as expanding social welfare programs, introducing entitlements, or amending taxation. There are dimensions to human agency and its valuation, such as individual reputability and relative position with the societal hierarchy, that are connected to but independent of both employment and wealth. Historical cultural factors will shape the 'society of leisure' as much or more than the impacts of the post-labor economy, with the effect that cultural difference is crucial to the shape of this emergent order: what works in one region or country may not work in another.

The existing cultural, economic, and political dominance by the managerial classes is supported by the nineteenth century "Protestant Work Ethic" that makes the human labor performed by lower classes essential to moral value: "idle hands are the devil's workshop."[13] This cultural ideology justifies the exploitation of the factory worker as a moral engagement of their time; idleness is despised and rendered immoral with both social and religious sanctions against it, making structural unemployment a source of psychological distress. These dualities are an expression of the same Enlightenment concerns with human agency that develops into the valorization of agency under industrialization. The equivalence between economic success and social position creates a nexus around the intellectual labor of reflective judgment: the creative intelligence common to both art and scientific discovery employed in the identification of 'laws' of nature—the idea of "first work" that enables practical applications—is ironically what allowed the invention of machinery that increased labor power by reducing the need for its intelligence and skill, facilitating the shift to automation. This force magnifier increases both the quantity and quality of facture, but the distribution of these products matches the imbalances maintained by capitalist economics reorganizing the differential order of Feudal society. The invention of automation does not alter these inherited contradictions, it reveals them, making their incompatibility obvious as an expression of Enlightenment ideals surrounding the appropriate role for agency. The 'great decoupling' represents the collapse of industrial and non-industrial work into the singular inchoate 'form of labor' that is the abstraction of agency–as–value as all productive activity. Yet the problem posed in these technologies is not the contradictions and paradoxes they reveal, but the difficulties confronting any attempt to organize the post-labor economy in a fair, equitable, and democratic way that creates a just society; justice is never guaranteed, even by the 'society of leisure.'

Issues of un/employment aside, the complexity, the challenges, and the opportunity for change offered by the proposition of a post-labor economy will require a fundamental reassessment of the social distribution of production, potentially reducing the alienation and exploitation of capitalism. However, in making this transition the established social questions of cost, access, and fairness continue to apply to all production–distribution interactions in the short-term as the older system passes and the new one comes into being. Yet AI poses unique problems for the *status quo* because it alters the *nature* of value itself, accentuating what has already been underway since the emergence of digital capitalism, visible as the shift to rentier currency begun in the 1970s; prior to this redefinition, historical currency was also a commodity in itself that functioned as the reified/saved values of past production by human labor. Historical value was an exchange of the value stored "as" commodities, rather than what it has become under digital capitalism—a title to demand *future* production not yet performed. In being a debt, it is a reified obligation that must be paid.

The invention of capitalism made possible by the industrial factory shadows Enlightenment ideals that valorized human agency. When AI replaces human agency, the resulting "value" created can no longer be attached to the productive action of human labor. Digital capitalism has already proposed a new model for value and exchange in this post-labor economy, but it has yet to address the more basic challenges of their distribution: *where will these titles to future production come from, who will receive them,* and *in what quantity?* How these questions find answers defines the cultural order of the 'society of leisure' as more or less *just* than that of historical capitalism. There is neither an obvious nor a given solution to these three questions about distribution, but the upheaval they entail is obvious and inevitable.

Rationalizing Intellectual Labor

Automation offers equal potentials for the invention of a new social order, or the hardening of the old order against change or challenge: like all technology, AI is a neutral mechanism that follows only the dictates of its construction, allowing its application to a contradictory array of roles and uses. The blunt nature of this force magnifier is apparent in how machine learning encodes the biases and structural inequalities inherent in the data used to create the AI, giving automation the potential to amplify existing injustices rather than correct them. This problem posed by algorithms is neither new, nor difficult to predict, nor even surprising upon even a moment's reflection because machines are instrumentalities for realizing human desires: not only in the form of production where the commodities answer to the demands that set the machine in motion, but in the transformation of those demands, in themselves, into commodities via pervasive monitoring, agnotology, and the marketing of "public relations." The development of "affect recognition" that registers emotional responses proposes to make this technology ever more persuasive.[14] These changes are simultaneously shifts in economic relations and evidence for cultural changes wrought by technology that were internalized by artists during the nineteenth century and the beginning of the twentieth. The avant-garde's concerns with *futurity* described by Italian art historian Renato Poggioli are a transformative shift in address from preserving past tradition to an orientation that calls a new order into existence.[15] A title to future production is nothing less than the right to demand that the performance of labor. The aesthetic emphasis on futurity anticipates digital capitalism's transformation of currency into an expression of futurity without material foundation[16] expands the cultural affinities between the expressions of art, the economic cycle of wages::profits, and the instrumentalities of facture.

The "free" production of autonomous machines provided online, as with the on-demand service provided by a search engine such as *Google, Baidu, Bing,* or *DuckDuckGo,* is a difference in degree only from immediacy of a "same day" delivery from *Amazon.* These processes reify the illusion of no (or very low) cost, no scarcity of commodities, and no limits to consumption that is the aura of the digital. The distribution of production is the issue that confronts the dominance of automated systems in the post-labor economy rather than their capacity to respond on-demand. But this shift to futurity undermines how Veblen describes wealth acting as a marker of social position:

> With the growth of settled industry, therefore, the possession of wealth gains in relative importance and effectiveness as a customary basis of repute and esteem. [...] It becomes indispensible to accumulate, to acquire property, in order to retain one's good name. When accumulated goods have in this way once become the accepted badge of efficiency, the possession of wealth presently assumes the character of an independent and definitive basis of esteem.[17]

The 'society of leisure' has always existed, but its membership has been highly restricted. It employs wealth as a marker of social standing: the ownership of commodities assumes a scarcity and difficulty for production that disappears with on-demand semiotic production, and is exacerbated by the transition from immaterial to material facture. With the abundance offered by an expansion of the 'society of leisure,' an accumulation of possessions ceases to be a reliable marker of status once that production ceases to be rare—commodity ownership ceases to act as a stand-in for position within societal hierarchies. This discrepancy is a reason why the rare and exclusive allure of art products remains high, even for works that are readily distributed through digital reproduction, such as the musical oeuvre of J. S. Bach which has enjoyed an increased reputation due to its availability via recordings.[18] The aesthetic refinement displayed by art is a cultural value independent of its commodity presentation. The ready availability of Bach performances enhances cultural distinction and status rather than diminishes it, increasing the demand for "real" experiences—actual live performances for example—rather than those mediated by technology apparent in the high ticket prices commanded by the most famous performers for their concerts.

Theorizing a post-labor economy presents a kaleidoscopic array of tendencies whose formations and fissures act to chart the challenges for accountability in autonomous systems and AI via how the machine reifies the ideology of digital capitalism.[19] Thus, criticism of AI requires an approach that is fundamentally theoretical, a recognition of its relationship not only to earlier machinery, but to the received ideas ratified in/as the apparatus itself, beyond any proximate problems posed by flaws in the particular data used to create these automatons. Questions about this post-labor economy are not merely an issue of machines, but of the social/cultural construction of human agency. Automation changes the Enlightenment obsession with human agency into the same instrumentality employed in the factory, and the invention of both weak and strong types of AI shows this obsession with the creation of a post-labor order for what it is: aspirations to re-establish a 'slave' society that emancipates the slave owners from any material concern with need; a social order where production is not dependent on human agency, but instead matches the caprices of desire, one that allows the exuberance of the 'society of leisure' to ultimately betray the Enlightenment ideals of rational and empirical thought.[20]

The issues that consistently return in these critical appraisals of automation are all interconnected by the issue of how automation challenges the existing order of society under digital capitalism. It is not a leveling of hierarchies that emerges from this technology, but rather a series of applications, each of which is a reification of ideologies forming multiple and overlapping impacts originating within the Modernist world born from the Enlightenment. This crystalline order, predicated on the exclusion of the impure in a fundamental denial of change, adaptation, and development stands in opposition to the "creative destruction" of the competitive marketplace.[21] Both digital capitalism and industrial capitalism alike are eminently Modernist products of Enlightenment thought that makes human agency a central concern of economic, political, and social organization by providing a system of ethical, religious and cultural norms that justify its oppressive and authoritarian tendencies. This cultural order, whether it is an aesthetic purified of all excess decoration and reduced to its essential core— claimed as a moral prohibition on waste—a fantasy of a state of nature untouched by humans—yet which requires ever increasing interventions to maintain the illusion of a nostalgic past—or a social construction of race, gender, sexuality—understands any deviation from the narrow selection or *a priori* acceptable options as pathology to be controlled, eradicated, and imprisoned. Utopia and Dystopia are equal fantasies of self-deception and comfortable vanity that obstruct any critial analysis of the contemporary problems posed by AI. Considering these cultural constraints and their significance offers a more complex understanding of how the transition to a post-labor economy restricts our capacity to reduce human misery, create a more democratic society, or redress the imbalances between wealth and poverty—the disparities of distribution and consumption for all things that are useful or agreeable, and which also possess exchange value.   Ω

§ 1. THE COMMODIFICATION OF AGENCY

The definition of capitalism in '**human agency traded as a commodity**' is a reflection of Enlightenment ideals of human action: a conversion of human intellectual ability into a *sine qua non* of production—with rational, logical thought considered the paragon of inventiveness and innovation. Enlightenment values are enshrined in economics as "Rational Choice Theory," the assumption that consumers know exactly what they want and never change their minds, make purely rational choices exclusively motivated by their own self-interest, and always have a complete access to any relevant pricing information. This positivist emphasis on human comprehension and ingenuity permeates the capitalist invention–deployment of technology; the industrial revolution was a literal 'proof' of its efficacy in the world. Thought–as–productive labor and its role in the creation of commodities has wrought a continuous instability for capitalist production. Each new, disruptive technology demonstrates the Enlightenment elevation of reflective judgment and the novel invention over the determinative application of knowledge, making the creation of "labor–saving" devices an inherent part of the capitalist enterprise. The machine that eliminates the need for human labor is the ideal expression of this rejection of work—technological unemployment and the post-labor economy are expressions of this ideology in application. However, the issue presented by both weak and strong AI is not whether digital automation will replace all human jobs, nor if these autonomous technologies will be a net creator of new jobs—both questions are short-term concerns that mistake proximate displacement for structural change: what matters are the cultural impacts the decentering of human agency in the production of value will have. The structural demand apparent in the law of automation, that *anything that can be automated, will be*[22] is not the same as a complete replacement of all human labor, merely the recognition that in digital capitalism wages are understood as lost profits. The 'intelligent labor' that AI displaces is simply a matter of determining which rule/law to apply—expert tasks that are simultansously performed with a minimum of conscious consideration.

Capitalism instrumentalizes Enlightenment concerns with enabling human efficacy in the world, a process that emphasizes the role of physical and intellectual labor in creating technology that magnifies human action. The industrial revolution became capitalism because of the need for a mass of human labor to operate these complex early machineries; yet over time each invention was replaced by a more efficient, more complex, and more profitable device in a series of industrial re-revolutions destabilizing even dominant businesses that do not continue to innovate and adapt to new technical developments. Human labor is a tangential concern, important only in terms of its intelligent role within these unintelligent machinic operations: the need for human labor in type and quantity changes with each new innovation, but never entirely disappears from *any* capitalist activity. Economist Joseph Schumpeter identified this overturning and replacement of business operations as "creative destruction" to explain the dynamic, constantly shifting competition for both resources and profits (surplus value) that has concentrated corporate power:

> [The] capitalist economy is not and cannot be stationary.
> Nor is it merely expanding in a steady manner. It is
> incessantly being revolutionized *from within* by new
> enterprise, i.e., by the intrusion of new commodities or new
> methods of production or new commercial opportunities
> into the industrial structure as it exists at any moment. Any
> existing structure and all the conditions of doing business
> are always in a process of change.[23]

Schumpeter is describing impacts of "disruptive technology" on the business cycle; however, the variability and shock this innovative drive creates within capitalism should not be mistaken for the constancy of its structural operations.[24] Old businesses being continually challenged by new businesses is only a superficial dynamism: the system of capitalism itself remains constant, largely independent of the Brownian motion generated by economic competition and innovative means of profit generation. Digital capitalism obfuscates this distinction between the proximate change of particular businesses or industries and the structural order that constrains and directs their behaviors; these differences are important to acknowledge when confronting the challenges posed by digital automation in general, and autonomous agency (AI) in particular. The intellectual component of facture, *agency,* is the difference between an automated process and an autonomous one: the automated process requires the oversight provided by human labor, an autonomous machine, by definition, does not require oversight once it has been set in motion. Cultural factors derived from the Enlightenment intersect with AI in a demonstration of impacts that are neither only economic, nor merely political, but social and philosophical as well: the capacity to render some forms of human cognition via an algorithm enables machine learning to exhibit the same distinction between reflective and demonstrative thought that Enlightenment philosopher Immanuel Kant used to separate the understanding of a concept from its fixed role in analysis. His understanding of judgment presents two potential approaches:

> The first alternative is rational and mathematical cognition through construction of the concept; the second is mere empirical (mechanical) cognition, which can never yield necessary and apodictic propositions. Thus I could indeed dissect my empirical concept of gold, and would gain from this nothing more than the ability to enumerate everything that I actually think in connection with this word; but although a logical improvement would thus occur in my cognition, no increase or addition would be gained in it.[25]

There is a distinction of type from cultural significance in Kant's proposal. Those judgments that follow a predetermined path dictated by existing rules (determinative judgment) can only employ the existing knowledge identified in the rule's creation, and are thus of lesser significance than creative thought that discovers new knowledge (reflective judgment); there is no novelty in the act of applying knowledge or employing an already-existing rule. The "mere empirical (mechanical) cognition" Kant describes is a literal description of how computers employ a database in semiotic production. The relevance for AI is explicit. Digital automation implements and manages information in a totalizing action that instrumentalizes the state of information as the range of potential *a priori* options known by the laws that a 'determinative judgment' applies; any AI system that is not capable of self-reflection and consciousness is also not capable of matching the role for human agency in rule creation (reflective judgment). Its relationship to art is self-evident: the rules of engagement are open to question in art.[26] These distinctions between rote and creative judgment that render Schumpeter's productive process capable of "conserving established positions and [...] maximizing the profits accruing from them"[27] mirror the immanence of autonomous agency and AI generally; it is a mechanism that demands all production be a set of limited outcomes established in advance—even when they have not been produced, they are potentially immanent—due to the range of responses the algorithm describes and by that describing, instrumentalizes.

The techne of AI is *not* what Kant identified as 'transcendental' analysis applied in the creative process of invention that is central to the Enlightenment's elevation of reflective thought, *nor* is it the innovations used in the "creative destruction" of Schumpeter's capitalism. Instead, the process of machine learning depends on a mechanical enumeration of elements—a cataloging—of material contained "in the mind." It derives rules that enable its function by analyzing existing data. In contrast to determinate cognition that employs existing knowledge as a given, the emphasis on innovation in capitalism matches the more important form of thought Kant describes: the creation of *new* concepts by reflective judgment (managerial decisions). The essential concern in capitalism with 'profit generation and maximization' simply identifies mechanisms that express this ideology: the survival of individual businesses instrumentalizes creative reasoning in the demand 'adapt to technological change or die,' which gives the elevation of this mechanism a logical inevitability. Simultaneously, the central ideological role of reflective judgment identifies the link between economic constraints and the societal hierarchy. The cultural analogues to the denigration of rote labor and the innovative challenges of disruptive technology converge in the rejection of *a priori* conditions that succeeded in the past: apparent in the cult of youth, the cyclic changes of fashion, and the promulgation of the art world's avant-garde—with its explicit manifestos, concerns for futurity, and nihilistic rejection of all received traditions.

§ 1.1 Distinctions in Automation

The issue with artificial intelligent is not how smart or dumb, weak versus strong the AI mechanism is, but how its operative translation of human agency is consistently an issue of rationalism personified: all types of AI employed in production are purely logical and pursue strictly fixed, determinate ends, but lack self-volition; they are not conscious. Although the technology that makes these devices possible, machine learning, is a force magnifier more potent and dynamic than previous technologies, those automated systems that require human agency, behaving as augmentations of human labor, do not promise the same scope of transformative displacement that both weak and strong AI that eliminate human labor necessarily do. The range of these digital systems that automate intelligent behavior overlap with those that automate human agency: programs that perform complex actions in direct response to human oversight, such as the generative production of a commodity designed by human action, occupy one extreme in a range bounded at the other end by those machines that perform complex actions without human oversight, such as driving a vehicle in traffic to a particular destination. This second type of autonomy seemed insurmountably complex as recently as 2004.[28] Although both types of digital automation have a powerful degree of convergence in their relationship to human oversight and the automation of intelligent tasks, they are not the same thing. An automated system that responds to and facilitates human actions, such as a *Snapchat* filter that transforms faces on demand, is qualitatively different than speech, facial, and affect recognition software that operates continuously, or the self-driving, autonomous vehicle that goes to a destination without requiring human instructions, even though all three systems fall at different points within the same range of autonomous, unintelligent functioning. While this shift in technical potency is an intensification of earlier shifts to mechanization and the replacement of human labor begun during industrialization, automation that requires a human decision "merely" reduces the need for human labor; autonomous agency operating without oversight suggests a replacement of human labor *in toto* by digital systems. Automation in general may produce the some of the same social impacts as the autonomous agency of AI, but their relationship to human agency separates them into mutually exclusive extremes:

[1] Automated systems that *reduce* the need for human oversight, amplifying human agency and enhancing human productive actions without replacing them.

[2] AI systems that *fully replace* human agency with algorithmic functions, entirely eliminating the need for any human labor in the task being automated.

Considering the potential cultural and economic impacts of these two types of automation makes their distinction essential: not all digital automation produces the same social displacements, nor challenges the creation of value in the same way, although both varieties of automation *do* replace human workers with a lower cost, more efficient system that is also much more productive; context for the labor being replaced determines the utility of this automation, a factor that shows the capriciousness of pervasive monitoring's speech and affect recognition via the problems of significance and reliability that limit every AI's productive capacity for tasks focused on signification.[29] However, digital automation is a powerful force magnifier that exponentially increases the amount of labor power available to a single person using computer technology; it dwarfs Schumpeter's proposal of "creative destruction"[30] at an ever expanding scale unimaginable in his lifetime.

The socio–economic impacts of AI arise from replacing human agency in specialized "knowledge work" or intellectual labor. Automation subjects those expert fields that were posed as replacements for the automation of physical labor to the same reductive, abstracting process that displaced factory works by simplifying the tasks they performed; autonomous agency replaces intellectual labor by transforming expertise into a fixed set of rote conditions that do not require reflective judgment. The social, cultural and political disruptions accruing to AI are specific to the automation of intelligent action, a replacement of human labor that is more than an amplification of existing productivity, but which originates with the capacity of weak and strong AI systems to replace a large, human staff with a single computer. The necessity to distinguish between amplifications of human agency and autonomous agency becomes apparent in the 'great decoupling' where digital technologies produce a separation between worker productivity, the number of employees required for production, and the growth of their wages in relation to that production—while expanding the scope of jobs impacted by automation to include the formerly resistant-to-automation labor of skilled professionals.

Digital capitalism manipulates data in a spectrum of complex and intelligent behaviors that do not require understanding for their performance: Kant's description of a mechanical operation to "enumerate everything" is easily applied to the automation of most mundane intelligent labor that requires skill but not creativity. This re-conceptualization of intellectual labor as a fixed application of 'rules' makes the connections between machine learning and immaterial labor explicit. The operation of any AI is a "proof of function" that acknowledges how all automatons literalize *Conceptual artist* Sol LeWitt's comment that "the idea becomes a machine that makes the art."[31] The creation of the database (Kant's "catalog of concepts") and its operations are rote processes that do not arrive at new systems of understanding, even if they do invent previously unknown arrangements and find new patterns in already existing data. Their action reconfigures a set of known potentials. Semiotic production precisely matches these capabilities of the database that are syncretic rather than inventive. They manipulate similarities and convergences, but do not create *new* knowledge. The difference between the creative action of reflective judgment linked to signification and those defined by mechanically following rules is apparent in games. The board game *Go* is defined by a precise, limited set of rules employed by fixed and determinate operations that contains a highly complex set of potential moves, but is also bounded by the consistent application of the 'rules.' The technical challenge posed by playing the game is distinct from the philosophical demonstration the AI system *AlphaGo* provides: the number of potential moves in *Go* creates the appearance of complexity, but it remains governed by a limited set of discrete rules that map all the potential moves in advance—even if the number of potential movies is too large to physically calculate, the machine still follows the internal dictates of its programming established by those *a priori* guidelines. *AlphaGo* demonstrates how rules impose a determinate process, realized in its automated judgments about the *Go* game board after each turn that determines which move to make to lead to a victory. What matters in any AI system is the determinate nature of problems the machine addresses; the guidelines for achieving victory are what *AlphaGo* learned, demonstrating the *a priori* containment-by-rules that makes the automation of gameplay possible.

Translating human agency into a fixed protocol makes the cultural valuation of judgment an essential issue for understanding the significance of autonomous agency: *AlphaGo* is no more aware of its victory than an alarm clock understands the time when it is supposed to sound an alarm—at the appointed moment the alarm sounds, the machine achieves victory; it does not understand the importance of its action. Training the neural network of an AI such as *AlphaGo* allows the 'discovery' of empirical laws contained by the data that trains it using a feedback loop which then directs its continued operation, but in doing so it reifies judgment as a protocol apart from reason or intelligence that separates significance from form: when its programming works properly, *AlphaGo* wins the game; victory in playing *Go* is a demonstration of correct processing. The human agency that created the rules continues to dictate the results for even a fully autonomous system such as *AlphaGo*. The central question to ask of these machines is: *Whose judgments are being automated?*

The autonomous functioning of AI places it outside of human oversight, a fact already apparent in the robust incontestability that blocks challenges to algorithmic systems once they are implemented: the response "computer says no" is simultaneously an observation of technical results and a deferral of responsibility—agency—to mechanical processes beyond the individual's control. These intelligent operations encoded by machine learning are a manifestation of received dicta not readily open to question, debate, or investigation by outside observers.[32] This dimension of emergent rules derived from the data employed in 'training' an AI hampers any critique of autonomous agency. However, these systems are not legal frameworks but machinic instrumentalities whose use acts to replace social, legal, and economic relations with the imaginary objectivity of a machine. AI creates a series of structural oppositions and ideological lacunae emergent at the intersection of digital capitalism's demands with the requirements of the social that constrain the implementation of AI:

[1] The opposition wages::profits that becomes apparent in the use of machinery, automation, and AI as an extractive means to concentrate surplus value by eliminating human labor costs.

[2] Immaterial semiotic production creates potential value through manipulations of the database reveals a contradiction with the social demand for utility (use) that limits exchange.

[3] Human agency poses a parallel limit on valorization apart from utility, both as an activator of digital processes, and as

a subject whose actions generate value via
pervasive monitoring.

[4] The proposal of social credit systems administered by
AI renders the established societal hierarchy resistant to
challenge, converting the inherited privileges of the *status
quo* into a fixed social order.

[5] The difference between material utility and social utility,
apparent in the ways that societal hierarchies depend on
the "waste" of value to demonstrate social position opposes
universal basic income as a solution to automation
eliminating the need for human labor.

These impacts are directly or indirectly linked to how digital objects
create profit. Valorization of autonomous agency challenges social,
economic, and political orders to potentially disrupt a societal hierarchy
based on wealth display and acquisition. These contradictions are not
dialectical: they identify paradoxes and mutually exclusive demands
that link how every AI application meets and reflects economic and
cultural impacts back upon their ideological sources, revealing them.
Interactions between capitalism and the social are not new; neither are
they surprising unknowns. The shift to the immaterial production made
possible by autonomous agency converges on the historical lineage of
disruptive technology in industrial capitalism.

Creating a framework for thinking about human agency in relation
to AI depends on understanding the social meaning and cultural role of
the intelligence being addresses. Automation that accentuates human
action has a parasitic dependence of human agency for its operation
and thus does not pose the same challenges as a fully autonomous
agency does. The distinctions in agency between that of management
(design) and labor (production) are important to acknowledge as a
fundamental feature of the cultural ideologies that inform both types
of digital automation. The invention of machine learning that results
in autonomous agency (AI) is the creation of a prosthetic agency, a
maximization of the managerial capacity that directs and controls
production (i.e. a force magnifier), without requiring the human agency
of labor for the facture itself, a distinction that links the AI system to
the labor of slaves and other production performed by 'insignificant'
human labor in the past, but offers the potential for a more egalitarian
'society of leisure' that reduces misery, poverty, and deprivation.

§ 1.2 Taylorist Foundations

Automation displaces labor in an ongoing process that is hidden by the aura of the digital. The capitalist ideology that values disruption as a metaphysical or transcendent creation acts to erase the connections between historical physical production and the immaterial production, thereby continuing the historical domination of human action and agency beyond the limited bounds of the assembly line.[33] Digital automation is already performing routine tasks with little oversight; AI accelerates the eclipsing of social, legal, and political mechanisms, replacing them with autonomous, generative systems that operate without the need for human control. Earlier mechanical systems anticipate this replacement of human intelligence with the computationally-intensive activity of digital systems through the cultural disdain for the agency of anyone but the capitalist who directs production. It is an attempt to automate the process of growing earnings by eliminating human labor from the costs of production.[34]

Supplanting the human intelligence required in production is not only a fundamental principle of the regimented assembly line and scientific management, it is also the conceptual source for the compartmentalization and fragmentation of tasks in/by automation. This isolation of labor from making decisions defined industrial mass production in the first half of the twentieth century, became axiomatic for the cybernetic revolution of the second half, and is emergent in the twenty-first century invention of autonomous agency. Frederick W. Taylor's proposals in *The Principles of Scientific Management* (1911) isolates the role of intelligence from the activity employed in commodity production, a conversion of facture into an unintelligent activity that anticipates the development of AI systems:

> The work of every workman is fully planned out [...]
> describing in detail the task which he is to accomplish as
> well as the means to be used in doing the work.[35]

Taylor is instrumental in eliminating labor's agency from the manufacturing process. Machine learning replaces the planning process; once trained any AI can perform the designated task without requiring human oversight. The compartmentalization and abstraction of intelligent actions matches how scientific management removed labor's intelligence from the manufacturing process once that process has been articulated. Both weak and strong AI mirror the unintelligence of the fragmentary actions performed on an assembly line: this elimination shows that the shift from physical production to immaterial labor is a change of degree and kind, but not of methodology. Those tasks most readily automated by AI already resemble the repetitive nature of physical production: most skilled professional intellectual labor manipulates an esoteric set of rules, but produced only a limited number of predetermined outcomes that are dictated in advance by the rules; the skill of this labor lies with knowing when to apply the appropriate rule. As with the playing the game *Go*, this type of immaterial labor reflects a 'legislative' judgment that selects/applies a specific law or rule for/to a particular case. The expertise of intelligent labor lies with knowing *when* to apply the appropriate rule, a mechanical decision. The problem for the managerial control over complex systems such as *Go* is in deriving the rules that lead to victory, not their *a priori* existence. Machine learning accentuates Taylorism, maximizing divisions between the intelligent agency of management and the (un)intelligent actions of labor. It enables a fantasy where the vagaries and discrepancies created by the mediation of human intelligence (what gives labor a degree of freedom for 'creativity of production' in implementing the work) are fully replaced with the decisions of management. For the assembly line, control is accomplished by regimented, fragmentary actions that allows human labor to be automated out of production entirely and replaced by a machine that only does what it has been told to do. Centralized control is always the goal.

Scientific management reflects a solipsistic view of labor and social order, one where unmanaged human agency is the enemy to repress or destroy; only those individuals with talents, ambitions, and desire for power and dominance (i.e. capitalists) matter. The transformation of human labor into discrete, fragmentary, and unintelligent moments in the production of commodities actively suppresses intelligent action by human labor and replace this intelligence with a rote, unintelligent process—the living labor that performs the actual work of production is reduced to either to being a parasite threatening the rightful orders of capital by begging for handouts, or to being a mindless mob following orders in exchange for privileges, however meaningless, offered by management. These industrial protocols anticipate William Ross Ashby's theory of cybernetics that is foundational for the development of computer technology;[36] the same transformations of more complex, intelligent tasks via machine learning enables their replacement by AI. With the force magnification of algorithmic functions made possible with AI systems, this technology affirms the illusion that highly specialized, skilled human labor is unnecessary. Digital capitalism amplifies/hides the consistent fragmentation of the assembly line that is accompanied by an ongoing elision of human agency reified as the instrumentality of AI: the aura of the digital as a magical domain, infinite, capable of generating value without expenditure, and allowing an ideological fantasy of production–without–human–labor to guide the conception of digital automation as an instrumentalization of managerial agency.

§ 1.2.1 Determinative Judgment

Autonomous agency has expanded the power imbalances between management and labor by devaluing human intelligence and expertise. Machines supplementing and replacing human action via autonomous or semi-autonomous systems of various types is neither new, nor particularly note worthy; what is significant about AI is not this replacement, but the categories of human labor being replaced—most obvious in those professional fields employing highly skilled, intelligent labor concerned with the manipulation of arcane culturally-defined systems bounded by explicit rules and laws. AI has already replaced the need for any human labor in simple tasks such as scheduling or validating information.[37] Concentrating managerial control as an immanent instrumentality presents an exponential magnification of labor force productivity by reducing the need for human agency in specifically immaterial labor, what Kant identified as "determinative judgments" in *The Critique of Judgment*:

> Determinative judgment [which operates] under universal
> transcendental laws given by the understanding, is only
> subsumptive. The law is marked out for it *a priori*, and
> hence it does not need to devise a law of its own so that it
> can subsume the particular in nature under the universal.[38]

Machine learning identifies general principles from the analysis of large databases; the application of these rules defines the production of AI because it specifically replaces human agency in tasks involving decisions made within a limited scope of potentials. It allows AI to deskill the expert whose special knowledge is simultaneously a routine manipulation of an esoteric set of conditions that only allow a limited set of correct actions. This narrowness of AI operations is immediately familiar to anyone who has needed to make a request that the system does not recognize; anything that does not 'fit' the *a priori* result is not allowed by the system itself. This common failing when interacting with autonomous machines in routine–but–intelligent tasks expresses the inflexibility of "rationalized" protocols when confronting ambiguity and ambivalence.

The replacement of human mental activity—intellectual labor—is a change of degree and of kind when compared to automating physical activity, but not of methodology: the automation of the *un*intelligent aspects of intelligent labor does not require comprehension or significance beyond the parameters of the rules themselves, evident in the continual expansion of automation into new fields that could not be automated in the past. Recognizing actions that formerly required the agency of living labor as products of a rote, 'determinative judgment' reveals these tasks were essentially *un*intelligent: they did not solve problems, merely perform actions according to a complex rule set. The continuity between the autonomous agency of AI and historical mechanized systems is apparent in their uniform replacement of rote actions by human labor. Any mundane, repetitive activity that can be reduced to a formal protocol where the results are identifiable in advance and subject to a rule set with only a limited range of potential outcomes is readily subject to automation—with the automation of determinative judgment, the costs of *all* living labor become barriers to profit generation. This convergence of professional and assembly line worker betrays the fallacy of factory workers retraining into the professional class: one type of routine production was replaced by another in a different setting, but no less mundane. The managerial decisions (reflective judgments) remain separate from the 'mere work' that is the primary surplus value generator.

§ 1.3 The Role of Refractive Judgment

What the automation of determinative judgment demonstrates is the central role of the initial sorting of information into significant and insignificant, the separation of signal::noise. Aesthetic judgment makes the need for this foundational division of attention obvious: we begin by talking about non-aesthetic features (specifically facts and concepts correlated with our observations) that bring certain features of the work to attention, while simultaneously rejecting other features as irrelevant.[39] These dynamics of immanence and invisibility define the passive judgment that resolves ambivalence into coherence: order imposed by sorting into categories directs attention and shapes the signification process. These problematics of identification make conceptualizing the importance of 'refractive judgment' essential, since it is both foundational and commonly ignored, yet is the crucial action that makes autonomous agency possible—the identification of what requires attention. Initial assessments of such basic "facts" as depiction and visual content mask the refractive action that transforms mere marks and shadows into imagery and depiction. Without an initial choice to impose order on an image no further consideration is possible. 'Refractive judgment' is the precondition for any higher level interpretation, whether determinative or reflective.

The paradoxical reversal of forms that emerges in the ambivalent play of representational content in the metamorphic image *All is Vanity* (1891) by American illustrator C. Allan Gilbert demonstrates the importance of refractive judgment as a prerequisite for coherence [Figure 1.1]. To recognize something in the world or in art first requires searching for familiar elements that allow its identification; only then can decisions about that thing proceed.[40] This nineteenth century

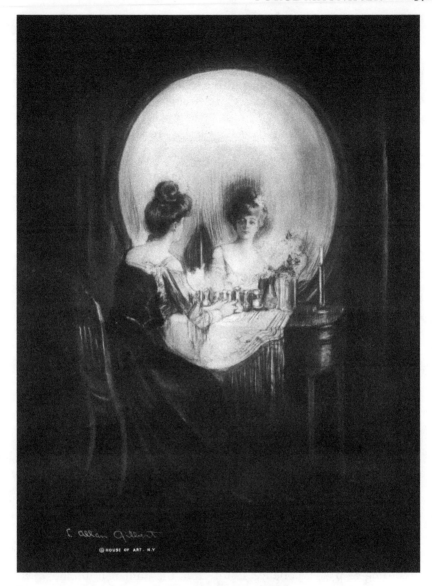

Figure 1.1: *All is Vanity*, by C. Allan Gilbert, 1891.

engraving exploits the ambiguity of human perception to create an unstable identification that manifests as a shifting between two very different compositions; recognition is overlaid with misrecognition in this optical illusion. *All is Vanity* forces our awareness of a specific type of judgment that precedes all others: the 'refractive judgment' that assigns category membership. It is an instantaneous decision that changes the image but alters nothing about it. This assignment of significance moves within distinct, superposed roles that compete for dominance in the assessment of what is seen: graphic lines and colored areas, discrete images of a woman and the room around her, and then again as a completely different image, a large expressionistic skull surrounded by darkness. Optical illusions are exemplars of the interaction between signal::noise that philosopher Jacques Attali explained in *Noise: The Political Economy of Music* as the central factor for coherent interpretation:

> With noise is born disorder and its opposite: the world. With music is born power and its opposite: subversion. In noise can be read the codes of life, the relations among them. Clamor, Melody, Dissonance, harmony; when it is fashioned by man with specific tools, when it invades man's time, when it becomes sound, noise is the source of purpose and power, of the dream—music.[41]

Attali's observation that "noise" is an absence of meaning separates the ambiguous and unknown play of things into significance and insignificance in an anticipatory judgment whose role is pure teleology, justified by the reflexive connection between the observational process and the particular "consistency of experience"[42] that directs it to coherence. These decisions are manifest in Gilbert's picture as the instability of its depictions: on one level they are just lines; while on another they create the woman, her vanity table, its contents, as well as the room; while on another entirely different level all these discrete elements lose their independence and combine to form the skull that surrounds/contains her. Which of these perceptions is correct, what is the "true" content of the image? All of them and none—its meaning depends on how they converge and combine: *All is Vanity*, a *momento mori* that is also a *vanitas*, a moralizing sermon on feminine deceptions concocted by make-up and perfume.

Determinative judgment identifies only the later decisions made possible by these initial recognitions that sort the encounter according to past experience: a link from the immanent-unknown to the already-known, a connection that is similar to the legislative act of determinative judgment, but distinct from the conscious choice that informs the determination and selects the appropriate *a priori* law.[43] The teleology initiated by category assignment does not require a knowledge of significance nor meaning, merely the process of using refractive judgment to impose a set of *a priori* givens which must be called into existence; before this act there is nothing to judge—no law, no image, no reality.[44] *All is Vanity* demonstrates the contingency of these interpretations, utterly different from the fixed outcomes of determinative judgment. Failure in this sorting disrupts all communication and coherence—Attali's concern with the order of music (signal) depends on this activity that discovers/invents its opposite, the inchoate nebula of "noise." The determinative judgments of AI arise from the discrete fragmentation of this refractive process: neither the judgment that assigns ambivalent experiences into categories, nor those categories in themselves constitute analytic conclusions, but are instead the precondition for them. Refractive judgment must resolve ambivalence before the determinations of an *a priori* dataset can operate: to say *All is Vanity* shows a "woman" or a "skull" depends on an initial decision about *what* that makes the determination—the recognition of the "woman" or "skull"—possible; it comes first, before applying the rule that teleologically identifies the contents: the category assignment process is fundamental—confusion about what is different and what is the same is confusion about everything[45]—the superposition presented by *All is Vanity* makes this confusion observable. The metastable imagery visible to human consciousness as discrete levels of interpretation reveals this process of identification in action.[46] Ironically it is the ambivalent and unstable contents of a metamorphic image that simultaneously "contains" several different pictures that demonstrates this role for refractive judgment in the rote and stable procedures of AI. The recognitions of *All is Vanity* creates a movement between within superposed, mutually exclusive configurations (the woman at her vanity, the leering skull) that arise from seamless shifts reorganizing the relationships of signal::noise into new configurations. It is a variety of visual poetry, as psychologist Mark Garrison explains:

> Poetry breaks the normative fantasy of perception because the poet and his audience remain constantly aware of the metaphorical character in his turns of speech. [...] The synaesthetic quality of ambivalence suggests that any turn of speech might have an ambivalent aspect.[47]

Meaning in poetry develops from associative patterns suppressed in 'normal' language, just as the duplicity of optical illusions are hidden in everyday visual experience. Unstable conception and recognition show refractive judgment is a conscious choice by the observer in how to look that defines the image contents: the "play" of poetic languages exists in relation to typical language; recognizing poetic language is a matter of agreement, "because the poet and his audience remain constantly aware of the metaphorical character"[48] employed by poetic language. The results of looking are apparent in the series of separate, overlapping, compositions corresponding to the familiar order of realism by evoking the familiar order of naturalism that matches each settled depiction to everyday experience.[49] Without a recognition of these ambivalences, the 'creative approach' is impossible; nevertheless it requires the 'normal' as a reference point, being precisely a divergence from everyday order. This difference is what makes the ambivalence of optical illusions useful in considering refractive judgment.

Automated agency reveals the foundational role of refractive judgment sorting experience/data in all later, higher-level decisions: the essential first stage in any judgment is the recognition that separates those conditions to judge (signal) against the range of insignificant elements to ignore (noise). This process is the coherence of everyday experience; apparent in those recognitions that correspond to 'normal' thinking, which are 'normal' simply because they are the most familiar solutions to the demands of an ambivalent and perceptually unstable world.[50] The foundational refractive judgment directs attention to particular details in the environment the require attention, thus agency. Our social identification of some human ideas as fallacious and others as correct, as well as the difference between pathological thought and 'normal' thought is a matter of degree, not of type,[51] arising from perceptual and environmental ambiguity "handled" by the interpreting mind.[52] The capacity to automate these initial judgments separates AI from other types of digital automation that require human assistance to perform these tasks. Those functions that identify materials are illustrated in the differences between two projects that both engage with facial recognition software for aesthetic purposes: Ethan Ham and Benjamin Rosenbaum's *Anthroptic* (2007) and Alexander Mordvintsev's *Deep Dream* (2015). Both art projects address the central importance of a specifically refractive judgment, but do so in very different ways that make the instrumental role of this foundational action obvious. Unlike the superposition of Gilbert's *All is Vanity* that exploits the ambivalence of human perception, these two projects demonstrate the fixity of image recognition in AI through its aberrant behavior. Computational analysis of large data sets makes the automation of human intelligence possible: these results are instances of "technesthesia"[53] where the imagery being identified does not correspond to a 'correct' match for human vision, but suggests instead a machinic fantasy or hallucination. Even in their 'failure' these machines remain directly linked to the instrumentalization of refractive judgment that renders a single result immanent.

Anthroptic uses a modified version of facial recognition software to search the online photographic database of *Flickr* in an attempt to identify images of its creator, Ethan Ham; however, he modified the software to cause it to misidentify faces. In a typical series of eight photographs, the program matched Ham's face to a cat, a tram [Figure 1.2], a flower, a section of an unidentified city, the *Public Market* sign in Seattle, the background behind a man drinking beer, and finally two pictures of faces, but not actual faces.[54] This process of mistaken identification

Figure 1.2: *By the Gondola ('IMG_1023' by Warren R.M. Stuart),* 2007;
   identified as a face by the AI program *Anthroptic;*
   image used with permission.

demonstrates the importance of the initial refractive judgment that separates those elements that becomes the 'face' from other details. The AI malfunctions. The higher level identification where seeing a known 'face' in the crowd (the *a priori* 'law') depends on the match between 'face' whose identity is not known to a 'face' whose identity has already been determined in advance can never begin. The refractive judgment for this AI divides signal::noise incorrectly, so the first step to identify the 'face' in each image glitches. What would merely be a determinative judgment demonstrates by its failure the interconnected roles of refractive and all later judgments as a sequential, dependent progression, each layer building on the earlier decisions.

Mordvintsev's *Deep Dream* directly shows this process of refractive judgment by transforming the analyzed image into a visualization of the identifications being made by the AI:

> One of the challenges of neural networks is understanding what exactly goes on at each layer. We know that after training, each layer progressively extracts higher and higher-level features of the image, until the final layer essentially makes a decision on what the image shows. [...] One way to visualize what goes on is to turn the network upside down and ask it to enhance an input image in such a way as to elicit a particular interpretation.[55]

The redrawn images have a wide range of appearances depending on the training imagery, but every example follows the same protocol of identification (refraction) and illustration of that identification by changing the scanned picture, as the "funny animals" generated by this system show [Figure 1.3]. Where Ham's project only provided a box that marked the identified 'face' in the image, Mordvintsev's project evokes the distorted dolls of photographer Hans Bellmer, the collaged body imagery of Pierre Molinier, or even the biomorphic imagery of Salvador Dalí's paranoiac critical method, but without creating metamorphic illusions.[56] This link to a 'metaphysical reality' demonstrated in Surrealist aesthetics[57] (and visionary art generally) is made explicit by the project's title. Automating the separation between the refractive judgment that identifies what is to be assessed in *Deep Dream*, and the determinative judgment that applies a known rule derived through machine learning to that decision reveals how AI allocates attention to details (which, where) dictates judgment itself: the initial decision about what is "seen" prescriptively determines the results (the art) of its productive application. Both artistic adaptations of image recognition software exploit its failings and errors (glitches) to bring the operation of that system into conscious consideration, but it requires a human audience to pass an aesthetic judgment on this result,

"Admiral Dog!"   "The Pig-Snail"   "The Camel-Bird"   "The Dog-Fish"

Figure 1.3: *Funny Animals* generated by the *Deep Dream* system, 2015;
    licensed by *Google, Inc.* under a Creative Commons Attribution 4.0
    International License.

engaging the generated results in ways that are utterly impossible for
the unintelligent processes of AI that produced them, a reminder that
aesthetic judgments are bounded by social and traditional functions.

§ 1.4 Semiotic Production

Semiotics is a formal discourse of linguistic structure and form that
anticipates the same fragmentation, recognition, and manipulation
employed by refractive and determinative judgments in digital systems.
The convergence of semiotics and determinative judgment is immanent
in their similarity, marked by the centrality of refractive judgment as
the initial dividing of perception into signal::noise. Thus to say the
autonomous systems of digital capitalism are semiotic is not merely a
metaphor: first as operations performed on and by coded languages,
and then again as a transfer of those determinative judgments created
by predefined outcomes that are known but awaiting recognition in
application, thereby allowing a computational generation of potential
values proposed by this internalized rules system. The 'fixed' range
of correct formulations posed by language allows its manipulation
without reference to its significance, a separation of formal lexical order
from the nuances and ambivalence created by meaning.[58] Algorithmic
automation depends on the same formal arrangement of fixed elements
remaining within predefined limits for their operation. What machine
learning creates during training corresponds to the same operative
protocols of refraction and matching to rules/identification that are
employed by semiotic analysis.

Insights from semiotics are therefore relevant to understanding the
production performed by autonomous machines. The formal divisions
between sign (meaning carrier), signifier (its component elements), and
signified (the meaning itself) describes human language as discrete
functions whose *a priori* potential order creates meaning through its
connection to past experience.[59] For most written and spoken language,
this relationship results in a determinative judgment of meaning, but

in poetic and other types of explicitly ambivalent language such as allegory, only reflective judgment can understand its significance.[60] The determinative application of the applicable rule is also a matter of selecting the appropriate form of judgment to assess the statement. In creating order the result also justifies its use—a teleological understanding of lexia that compartmentalizes its formal organization via 'laws' of assembly independent from signifying processes, a fact that allows semiotic analysis to address questions of structural order without necessarily also considering the issue of any particular statement's meaning for its human audience. This separation of significance from arrangement also enables the unintelligent processes of immaterial facture characteristic of AI to manipulate lexia and linguistic forms without requiring their comprehension.

Describing the digital computer as a "semiotic machine" precisely captures the unintelligent aspect of its automated agency that belongs to a range of processes of where substitution, replacement, variation, and combination can proceed according to established and known laws without the necessity for the significance of those statements directing the result: a separation of the formal construction of signs from their encultured significance. Roland Barthes anticipates this compartmentalization process familiar from the assembly line and digital automation in his observations about pre-linguistic elements fragmenting and combining to produce significance:

> Distance and proximity are promoters of meaning.
> Everything proceeds from spacing out or staggering of articulations. Meaning is born from a combination of non-signifying elements (phonemes, lines); but it is not sufficient to combine these elements to a first degree in order to exhaust the creation of meaning: what has been combined forms aggregates which can combine again among themselves a second, a third time.[61]

The issue is not the meaning of individual terms, nor even their role in statements, but their de/composition into primary elements that provide structure to signification. In writing, both the components of letterforms and their identification as individual letters, as well as the arrangement into words, then statements matches this process. In *All is Vanity* those identifications that become a "woman" or a "skull" are what define the reflective judgment of content. These multiple levels of dis/assembly suggests the same compartmentalization used in all assembly line processes; refractive judgment identifies how the contingent scaling process moves from elemental units into significance following rote rule systems—for language these are the laws of grammar. However, significance (meaning) is not merely a product of following a set of prescribed rules (a determinative judgment), but is also a matter of subjective and irrational nuance productive of new concepts (a reflective judgment) that escapes from the containment of expectation, much as poetry refuses to match the established rules of grammar or significance.

Ambivalence defines the poetic statement, bordering on nonsense through its suspension of everyday coherence. The complexity of statements such as Noam Chomsky's grammatically correct, but nonsensical *"Colorless green ideas sleep furiously."*[62] offers an example of lexical ambivalence and ambiguity whose considered meaning evades easy comprehension: it can be understood as an example of nonsense, or as poetic contradiction, or even as a Gödelian inconsistency in the grammar of language, but not all three at the same moment. These meanings are not a product of the words—they reside in the capacity for a 'poetic function' apart from lexical order that creates the same appearance of profundity as in other meaningless statements such as "Hidden meaning transforms unparalleled abstract beauty."[63] Each interpretation is mutually exclusive; the range they propose has superposed potentials that transform into immanent–yet–contingent meanings depending on the particular frame of reference employed in the initial refractive judgment that assigns the appropriate domain for the higher level interpretations.

The instability of Chomsky's statement merely violates the human demand for coherent signification; there is nothing 'wrong' with it grammatically making it possible to translate into other languages. Understanding how a text becomes untranslatable makes the semiotic operation of digital systems apparent through the role of determinative judgment in the difficulties of translation. This alignment of the semiotic procedures of digital technology with an established, familiar order determines the outcome *a priori*. Marcel Duchamp's Francophone puns in his only completed film, *Anémic Cinéma* (1926) makes this 'translation problem' explicit. The texts in his film depend on the discrepancies between spoken and written French, as well as their visual juxtaposition with the imagery of the film for their meaning.[64] It draws attention to the difference between mundane statements and the allusive, intertextual orders of both art and poetry: the 'nonsense' in Chomsky can be translated, but the 'nonsense' in Duchamp cannot. The impossibility of the grammatically correct statement that Chomsky offers as 'nonsense' emerges not from a problem with its construction, but directly as a result of its interpretation—this distinction is central to acknowledge in considering his example. 'Poetic' meaning is not merely a process of indexing a term within a lexicon of past usage and grammatical structures; these problematics are specifically what the semiotician Roman Jacobsen has termed the 'poetic function' of language.[65]

Anémic Cinéma is an example of Duchamp's attempt to reclassify art as an intellectual activity, a change of conceptual address from purely visual form into the mental realm.[66] What he terms the "retinal art" of painting lies in a formal concern with imagery, rather than being addressed to religious, philosophical, or ethical/moral concerns.[67] This film is made from a combination of optical illusions (animated, spinning graphic patterns that spring into apparently 3D towers/tunnels) alternating with French texts; however, the statements in *Anémic Cinéma* are not purely lexical. They are simultaneously composed from the familiar structure of language and put into rotary motion like the spirals they accompany. This doubling of text::image makes these words especially difficult to translate, as film historian P. Adams Sitney explains:

> Something else happens [in *Anémic Cinéma*] when we begin to allow the puns to have their play. The figurative meaning of *"la moëlle de l'épée"* and *"le poêle de l'aimée"* over powers the literal (non)sense. The reference to sexual intercourse could hardly be more evident. [...] The sexuality is neither in the literal meaning of the words, nor represented in the optical illusions, seen by themselves.[68]

The meaning of the texts in *Anémic Cinéma* is neither a quality of the language, nor a product of the optical illusions, but both. It creates a quandary for interpretation by rendering the significance of these statements as something other than their lexical organization, a poetic excess whose recognition requires reflective judgment to understand. What Sitney recognizes about the sexual subtext to Duchamp's puns is an overlay of significance from verbal to visual and back again, an additional significance that is not present in the words themselves, but must be read into them allegorically from the actions of the imagery, which is then tautologically re-interpreted by the emergent sexuality of the texts in a self-reinforcing cycle. This process transforms both language and visuals in a way the exceeds the capacity of any translation to address what happens in the irrational, ungrammatical language of these puns:

> *Bains de gros thé pour grains de beauté sans trop de bengué.*
> *L'enfant qui tète est un souffleur de chair chaude et n'aime pas le chou-fleur de serre-chaude.*
> *Si je te donne un sou me donneras-tu une paire de ciseaux?*
> *On demande des moustiques domestiques (demi-stock) pour la cure d'azote sur la côte d'azur.*
> *Inceste ou passion a coups trop de famille, à coups trop tirés.*
> *Esquivons les ecchymoses des Esquimaux aux mots exquis.*

Avez-vous déjà mis la moëlle de l'épée dans le poêle de l'aimée?
Parmi nos articles de quinquillerie par essence, nous
  recommandans le robinet qui s'arrête de couloir quand on ne
  l'écoute pas.
L'aspirant habite Javel et moi j'avais l'habite en spirale.

These statements are functionally untranslatable because their meaning depends on the *sound* of the words; the "word plays" enact a double meaning which becomes apparent to French speakers when read aloud, communicating a complex significance that is *not* present in these spiraling texts and cannot be linked to their direct lexical definitions (when they are actual words and not misspellings). The obstacles raised by/to signification in Duchamp's film are a special case that demonstrates how the role of human interpretation limits the utility of determinative judgment in addressing the *a priori* relationships of language; Duchamp's statements simply do not follow familiar, grammatical rules. They are built from misspellings that create alliteration, puns that exploit differences between spoken and written French—simply translating them to their equivalent in another language is impossible. Ambivalence and allegory defeat translation, becoming coherent through the "decoding" made possible by the juxtaposition of text and image, but any translation necessarily loses this word play that is so important to the affect and significance in *Anémic Cinéma*, effectively denuding this use of language of its peculiar quality and losing a major part of its meaning as a statement.[69] This transformation of significance recalls the objection Duchamp has to "retinal art" does not lie with the optical experience, but with the issue of mental engagement in what the visual experience signifies: *Anémic Cinéma* is a perverse semiotic system where the visual achieves a linguistic function, and the graphic arrangement of the words becomes a source of meaning, as in visual poetry.[70] It insinuates a semiotic art dependent on a reflective judgment that renders texts as objects guided by context, allegory, and intertextuality. These added dimensions of signification are more important than the words in themselves, a fact that demonstrates the translation problem clearly: no two sentences in different languages can be fully equivalent.

The nonsense of *Anémic Cinéma* is entirely different in character and interpretation from Chomsky's grammatically correct, but meaningless statement that *can* be translated using an automated system such as *GoogleTranslate*: in French, his statement is *"Les idées vertes incolores dorment furieusement"*; in German it is *"Farblose grüne Ideen schlafen heftig"*; in Spanish the same statement becomes *"Las ideas verdes incoloras duermen furiosas."* In each translation the results retain the same *in*coherence because the statement exploits the structure of meaning in language (signification) rather than its formal appearance (signs). The grammar is correct and consistent with meaningful statements, a fact that makes the parallelism posed by translation from one language into another not only possible but remarkably self-similar. This lexical complexity originates with the impossible meaning of its terms, but it is readily translatable. For mundane speech that follows familiar forms and does not invoke a poetic organization, machinic translations may be interchangeable, but artworks such as *Anémic Cinéma* demonstrate the limits of semiotic production in systems such as *GoogleTranslate* where rote transpositions employ a database made from similar examples, rather than being derived from an understanding of the significance of the statements.

Because the poetic function of language is rare and most common statements closely follow the parameters of rote expectation, AI can parse and automate language-based problems—such as translation—as a matter of computational power and database complexity, rather than signification. The machine does not need to understand the meaning and nuance of human language to translate between languages for these everyday statements since they are bounded by rule sets that dictate assembly, correct arrangement, and formal presentation. These capacities are simply an expansion of earlier, commonplace systems such as spell check and grammar check in word processing software; both mechanisms ultimately depend on the same process of comparison of one immanent text with the contents of a database. A routine shift between one language and another is significantly more complex than correcting spelling mistakes, yet they fall within the same range of semiotic processing made possible by the transformation of language into a set of formal rules discrete from the lexical encoding of significance. The meaning of the text does not matter for these types of autonomous translation since the rules of grammar and index of terms function without reference to the coherence of the statements they create—as the differences between statements by Duchamp and Chomsky demonstrate.

§ 1.5 Automating Judgment: *Autonomous Agency*

Both determinative and reflective judgments are entirely different even though they begin with the same *refractive* judgment about *what* is being considered. While Kant notes "judgment in general is the ability to think the particular as contained under the universal,"[71] the differential between those judgments that are contain by established rules, and those that proceed to invent new rules operate as different types of understanding. This distinction becomes obvious in the unintelligent nature of weak and strong AI apparent in their subservience to established rule sets. This distinguishes the judgments subject to autonomous agency from what Kant terms "reflective judgments" that identify the universal (transcendental) order that defines the immanent:

> Hence reflective judgment, which is obliged to ascend from the particular in nature to the universal, requires a principle, which it cannot borrow from experience, precisely because it is to be the basis for the unity of all empirical principles under higher though still empirical principles, and hence is to be the basis that makes it possible to subordinate empirical principles to one another in a systematic way. [...] That does not mean that we much actually assume such an understanding (for it is only reflective judgment that uses this idea [of universal natural law] as a principle, for reflection rather than determination); rather, in using this principle judgment gives a law only to itself, not to nature.[72]

Reflective judgment creates rules, but is also independent of the rules it creates: significance is not a given—it must be invented. Human agency arises *sui generis* in response to unitary problems without the *a priori* limitations provided by already-knowable outcomes in a process where transcendental principles become the subject of thought, a creative process of imposing order and form; this realization is the definition of "genius" in his philosophy. Devising significance escapes from the limitations of immanent resemblance to past experience to describe the structural arrangement—it is a matter of design rather than recognition. In contrast to reflective judgment that depends on consciousness, the unintelligence of AI becomes obvious when considering how determinative judgment is constrained to matching a novel situation with the established information of the database; automation legislatively links the results of *refractive* judgment to already-knowable outcomes. The problems that remain relevant for human agency in a society where determinative judgment is performed by AI are precisely those decisions not subject to this *a priori* knowing: activities associated with invention and design—philosophical, poetic, moral, artistic questions without *a priori* answers—those activities whose performance is inessential to sustaining mere existence and have historically been associated with the higher ranks of the societal hierarchy, as Thorsten Veblen explains:

> From the days of the Greek philosophers to the present [early twentieth century], a degree of leisure and exemption from contact with such industrial processes as serve the immediate everyday purposes of human life has ever been recognized by thoughtful men as a prerequisite to a worthy or beautiful, or even a blameless human life.[73]

The rejection of human labor and material production is a signifier of the highest ranks of the societal hierarchy where mental activity concerned with invention and discovery—reflective judgment—is the only concern that matters. The dominance of those tasks associated with Veblen's "leisure class" creates the 'society of leisure' because AI removes the material costs of entry that historically served as the gate keepers of class distinction, democratizing its emphasis on the labor of reflective judgment through economic necessity.

All the well known potentials for significant displacements, social upheavals, and economic disruptions that are the proximate, short-term impact of autonomous agency does not alter its longer-term impacts on the cultural roles for productive activity: that once the large quantities of both highly skilled and unskilled labor have been displaced, AI will offer new ways for individuals and small groups to engage in creative production that was historically only available to industrial production. Automation reducing the need for human agency in production does not negate human agency's role in directing that production: all AI systems have a parasitic relationship to human needs ratified as valid via exchange. The invention of autonomous agency is a symptom of this new, emergent 'society of leisure' where design dominates value creation by eliminating the drudgery of production, allowing the artist to create with only limited concern for material execution, impacts already becoming apparent in some creative fields such as animated motion pictures.[74] This expansion of access and lowering of costs are nothing new; technological change has lowered entry costs for decades: these general shifts are already apparent in the use of digital automation for tasks such as animation: the labor that would require a studio and a large staff to produce can now be rendered in real time by a single artist working alone.[75] This technological change has revealed a three-tiered society composed from separate groups that can and often do overlap, but which comprise distinct power imbalances that become important with the invention of autonomous agency:

[1] *The bourgeoisie* who is the rent-seeker that owns and directs production; in digital capitalism this group is less often composed of discrete individuals than of investors and corporations. What is owned is typically a combination of intellectual and physical property, making this group deeply and literally invested in the continuation of the status quo and its maintenance against change.

[2] *The general population* who lack either expertise and/or have only limited access to the tools provided by digital systems, yet who are the primary subject of the

agnotology::surveillance dynamic, and whose wages are the foundation of the cycle of exchange value.

[3] *The technically fluent population* who can manage and employ the increasingly automated digital systems—who may be and often are employed by group [1] but who neither own nor control their production.

These three groups are obvious and readily identified. Their importance lies not with the novelty of this identification, but with how membership in each group is not a fixed and immutable division: they overlap—membership in one group does not preclude membership in another. Digital technology functions as a force magnifier as social access to productive technologies increases, a transformation that makes the conflict between ownership and utility apparent through rarified skillsets becoming commonplace, a change from rarified expertise to commodity. The challenges that AI poses for the social do not propose immediate and total upheaval, but will instead create an evolution of roles and functions as institutionally based power attempts to accommodate these developments.

In the case of animated motion pictures, a field that historically required extensive production crews and significant labor to produce even the shortest animated work, once that body of labor has been rendered an autonomous process, the issues around its valorization are neither the number of frames animated per second nor the limitations imposed by the technical skill of the staff making the drawings; instead the [1] managerial skill (design expertise) employed in deciding how the animation proceeds dominates its production, and the technical decisions recede in significance. As access and availability of digital tools increases, the instability of digital capitalism emerges as the permeability of groups [2] and [3]: only a small number of people belonging to the technically fluent population [3] are required for production, and as the digital tools become increasingly common and accessible they also require less expertise to operate even without being examples of AI systems. Once all productions are of equally high quality, their uniform execution insures that issues of aesthetics (style, novelty, interest, design) and significance (artistry) will dominate assessments of value—immaterial concerns with morphology and structure that are determiners of differences in qualia. These changes threaten the established process of valorization by increasing competition and making cultural uses the arbiters of marketability.

The collision between an historical system predicated on attempts to preserve existing values (the exchange of commodities) and the digital capitalism that valorizes the demand for immanent labor (titles to future production) does not disappear with the elimination of human labor by AI, it expands. Autonomous agency magnifies these conflicts between culture–as–commodity (production) and culture–as–social–praxis (utility). These dynamics make the question of valorization and the distribution of its benefits eminent as issues of societal hierarchy and the property relations attached to that order. Interconnected rifts divide these dimensions of production, consumption, and profit-seeking from one another—those fixed relationships assumed in the separation of activities that distinguishes management from labor. The instrumentalized control over access (DRM), the valorization of social activity, and the translation of societal hierarchy into an rigid system of privileges/allowances are all attempts to continue the historical profit seeking of digital capitalism beyond the transition to the 'society of leisure,' symptoms of how capitalists who have power will try and use it in ways to insure that they and their progeny retain it.

§ 2. CONFLICTS BETWEEN
LABOR, PROFIT, AND VALUE

The ideology of "autonomous achievement" develops in digital capitalism as the importance given to reflective judgment (the creative labor performed by management) and in the erasure of determinative judgment (the rote labor of production); it lends cultural authority to the progressive replacement of human labor with automation, and the digital expansion of this replacement by machine learning and autonomous agency. Replacing the routine-but-intelligent tasks performed by highly skilled professionals with strong AI impacts the organization of the societal hierarchy, but emerges as familiar structural oppositions within the political economy. Mismatches between human wages (labor), the creation of surplus value (profit), and the definition of capitalism itself in the externalization of human agency as a commodity exchanged for a wage are all features of industrial capitalism throughout its more than two hundred year history. These dynamics necessitate attempts to resolve the declining rate of profit described by the equation **surplus/(constant capital+variable capital)**.[76] The costs paid for all aspects of production (including human wages) reduce the rate of profits generated via exchange; as costs imposed by wages (variable capital) increase over time, the rate at which profits accrue declines, revealing a steady drop in surplus value generation that can only be countered by reducing the costs of wages through the shift to automation. The invention of AI is the most recent example of these ongoing attempts to increase profits by replacing human labor with machines; the reliance on semiotic production in digital capitalism is a variation on this attempt to solve the diminishing rate of profit. Simultaneously, the demand for growth in profits drives capitalist expansions into all unvalorized domains. These economics are both obvious and simplistic: businesses that do not generate surplus value—profit—go out of business. The "Luddite Fallacy," sometimes equated to technological unemployment, arises from these dynamics as the historically false belief that the jobs lost to machinery will not be replaced by other, new jobs that did not exist before. AI continues this opposition between labor and machinery inherited from industrial capitalism; however, both weak and strong AI puts the validity of this fallacy in question, since unlike historical machinery that augmented human agency, autonomous agency entirely eliminates it from both physical and intellectual labor, allowing the proposition of entirely eliminating human labor to be more than a fantasy. Whether AI actually creates a fully post-labor economy is unimportant; it is the even partial capacity to do so that poses the cultural impact.

Industrial machines lack agency, thus they required human labor; none of these historical systems make any judgments, refractive or otherwise. The impacts autonomous agency has on human society arise precisely from its automation of both refractive and determinative judgments. Displacement of the existing societal order is guaranteed by this change, since the 'commodification of human agency traded in exchange for wages' is the definitional moment in the emergence of capitalism. Understanding the structural barriers to this post-labor economy reveals the cultural impacts of how concentrated corporate power employs AI to maintain its cultural dominance, rate of profit, and the societal hierarchy.

§ 2.1 The Dynamics of Value Creation and Extraction

Exchange is a social function. It requires two parties by rendering their transfers of commodities/currency in a mutually acceptable reciprocity. This distribution of commodities is realized through the re/ circulation of wages/profits within human society. Capitalist value is socially created, not *from* past production, but out of human judgment reified in all production: commodities are the substance of value, but their foundation is human agency affirmed in production, and then again in the appraisal of *utility* that enables exchange. The automated agency of any AI reveals tensions in the assumptions of social interaction within historical capitalism and its valorization process. This basic proposal that commodities exist as values presupposes human agency and exchange to bring that value into existence, as Karl Marx noted:

> The labor time socially necessary is that required to produce an article under the normal conditions of production, and with the average degree of skill and intensity prevalent at the time. The introduction of power-looms into England probably reduced by one-half the labor required to weave a given quantity of yarn into cloth. The hand-loom weavers, as a matter of fact, continued to require the same time as before; but for all that, the product of one hour of their labor represented after the change only half an hour's social labor, and consequently fell to one-half its former value.[77]

Human labor is central to the operation of both the power-looms and hand-looms that Marx describes—yet it is not labor that produces value, but the mobilization of that production created through exchange: a social relationship that remains constant, entirely separate from the productive activity that creates the commodity itself. The value of hand-loomed production decreases for his analysis because it requires more labor to produce the same quantity of the commodity when compared to the volume produced by power-loom production. Consequently the industrial process disrupts the older technology, replacing it. This imbalance between labor and commodity production is what the shift to industrialization, automation, and AI all exploit: the way to increase the value created by exchange is to minimize the costs of labor required for producing commodities as by increasing the efficiency of that production in the shift from hand– to power-looms; however, the social reciprocity that marks commodities as valuable is also what sets the value available from exchange in a reversal where increasing the quantity of commodities produced paradoxically reduces the value of those commodities. Consider the case of printing a page of text: what required a week's labor in the 14th century is now autonomous, produced entirely on-demand by small machine that can sit on my desktop, an change that renders printing a page of text completely disposable. What was once highly valuable product of significant labor is now almost entirely worthless. The shift from valuable and labor-intensive productive activity to "free" reveals how automated productions devalorize the commodity. They have an ever decreasing value until their unit costs are subsumed into the general costs of the materials and machine itself. This progression makes the challenges posed by autonomous production palpable as it is a technology that will produce a fundamental reorganization of society. The cultural barriers to this development erected with digital capitalism are what will define the nature of those changes and who benefits from them.

AI's elimination of human agency reveals the wages paid to labor and the demands for profits by management are a structural contradiction in capitalism itself: the exchange relationship is a closed loop where the wages paid to labor return as the profits received from exchange for commodities, only to again become wages in a circulation that enables this process to continue. In this cycling of capital, the equivalence between wages, profits, and commodities is explicit; the concept of "surplus value" is simply a means to differentiate the proportionate excess that is "profit" from the full amount realized in exchange that repays what has already been expended.[78] (What matters is *spending*: who spends money, how much they spend, and what they spend it on—not the quantity of money in circulation.[79]) This paradox only apparently disappears with the shift to immaterial production and the semiotic facture of digital capitalism: its vanishing is an illusion created by the aura of the digital that redefines wages as lost profits by refusing to acknowledge the physical costs of facture, the unpaid infrastructural contributions of the social, or the essential economic cycle of capital turning wages::profits. Autonomous production enables purely extractive exchange that creates profits without wages, a looting of public resources that breaks this reciprocal spending within society, further concentrating corporate power through the consolidation of production without reference to the discharged workers who compose the market for commodities. This contradiction of AI and wages::profits is explicit: it withdraws the profits from recirculation by reducing/eliminating wage payments, or in a variety of rent-seeking changes in ownership, or both. This fact is apparent in the abandonment of the 'ownership model' for software (where it is purchased in the same way as other machinery) to a 'subscription model' that desublimates the extractive foundation of digital capitalism: AI performs a continual credential check to allow continued access/employment in production. Production itself becomes a commodity. This conversion is an expression of the historical managerial control over labor extended to *who* is allowed to operate these systems; it is a restriction of access to the productive apparatus. The cost benefits of replacing humans with machinery/software vanish, but this change does not reinstate the cycle of capital. The control imposed by digital rights management (DRM) converts the fixed cost of machinery/software into a variable cost that is *not* a wage paid to labor, generating the direct extraction that is rent. The aura of the digital and its fantasy of production–without–consumption hides the ways that renting software matches the historical costs of human labor in its continual growth over time. The productive means ceases to be a fixed cost, thereby eliminating the absolute benefit of investments in technology for the companies using these systems—a change that renders immaterial digital "machinery" (software) as a new form of unproductive extraction (rent) that benefits the creators of software, but not its users. This collection process is an allegorical model of how every AI extracts value from society as a whole: AI–as–labor is a privately owned resource that gives capitalists an absolute control over society through their ownership over commodity production essential to sustenance, matched by their accumulation of wealth that is not cyclically returned to society through wages.

§ 2.1.1 Use and the Scarcity of Capital

Unmooring production from the necessity/costs of human labor does not change the basis of exchange: surplus value generation is limited by social and cultural demands for utility (use) that was assumed in all historical types of production. The directness of this restriction on production makes its elision for AI an essential feature of how the aura of the digital disavows material limits. For historical capitalism there were structural barriers to the useless because it rarely produces profit since it does not generate exchange, making its facture unlikely since its costs become a pure loss or "waste" of resources, capital, and labor because without exchange there can be no surplus value. Semiotic manipulation valorizes all types of automation as a replacement for human labor in a fantasy–resolution to the conflict of wages::profits. This attempt to maximize surplus value in production through a reduction or elimination of 'variable capital'—the costs of human labor—unmasks the fallacy posed by autonomous systems:

AI does not maintain the rate of profit, which must still revert to human wages expended through exchange, and dependent on use.

The ways that AI and automation maintain their increased rate of profit is ultimately extractive: profits generated through automation necessarily devolve upon society as a whole, drawing capital away from other sources; this removal is the definition of "extraction." The aura of the digital hides this structural withdrawal in its elision of the physical from consciousness. Once there is no longer a human component, as in the already established semiotic production of the digital, the reciprocity between wages::profits becomes obvious in how commodity value emerges from its equivalence to human labor via the wages that become profits and the cyclic mobility of capital in society.

The immaterial production of machines makes the goal of all automation apparent; this transformation of the social realm into a commodity in digital capitalism is categorically different than the displacement of manual production by machinery. Nevertheless, the instrumentality of AI is a false mechanism for maintaining the rate of profit, much like the conversion of software into a variety of rent-seeking: semiotic production does not generate new values, only reconfigures past production as 'potential values' that await realization via exchange; their conversion to actual value removes capital from the cycle of wages::profits. These 'alternative' sources of profits are not new values, merely rearrangements those already in existence while adding titles to future production not yet performed, ironically creating a scarcity of capital when demands for production cannot be met. Even if automation does not completely replace human labor with the fixed costs of machinery, a reduction in labor costs is its fundamental goal; yet, as labor costs reach zero, this reduction in costs also devalues the commodities produced, as the desktop computer printer demonstrated—its costs are the materials used in its operation, not the printing it performs—a factor that makes maintaining the rate of profit increasingly difficult as AI becomes more central to production.

§ 2.2 Determinative Judgment, Human Labor, and Agency

The historical accommodation of the social to industrial production created a dependence on industrialization for all aspects of life. This change in societal organization is the most obvious impact of the shift from craft labor to industrial factories during the nineteenth century. It marks the cultural start of Modernism in art and design, as well as the transition from a Mediaeval and Feudal social order of rights and obligations that dictated labor, to the regimented organization of human labor as an independent commodity in itself. Established power asymmetries continue to shape society even though the nature of that society changes. These oppositional roles of conception and execution within capitalist production become explicit in the twentieth century with the restricted freedom of action evident on the assembly line. The same divisions inform *Conceptual Artist* Sol LeWitt's comments on the process of art–making in *Sentences on Conceptual Art* (1968):

> 28. Once the idea of the piece is established in the artist's mind and the final form is decided, the process is carried out blindly. There are many side effects that the artist cannot imagine. These may be used as ideas for new works.

> 29. The process is mechanical and should not be tampered with. It should run its course.[80]

The crux of his discourse is the relationship an avant-garde artist has to the breadth of art history; he suggests the artist's role is to create the boundaries (rules or conventions) necessary for working, a proposition that makes the connections between *Conceptual Art*, computer software, and the valorization of managerial agency in directing production (design) apparent as different variations on the same ideology. LeWitt's comments match the Enlightenment's emphasis on elevating reflective judgment and distinguishing it from determinative judgment, a separation proposed by Kant in *The Critique of Pure Reason*, that finds reification in the literally productive operation of machinery, or the activity of skilled fabricators making the objects designed by Conceptual and Minimalist artists. The same unintelligence of labor in executing an already created design that LeWitt describes for *Conceptual Art* is equally immanent in both the Taylorist protocol and Ashby's cybernetics where the instructions dictate the production as an *a priori* exercise. The *Sentences on Conceptual Art* directly evoke this design process as predestination:

> 6. If the artist changes his mind midway through the execution of the piece he compromises the result and repeats past results.

7. The artist's will is secondary to the process he initiates from idea to completion. His willfulness may only be ego.[81]

The irony of his proposal for *Conceptual Art* is that intelligent action is strictly contained in the initial creative phase of art design and eliminated from the fabrication process, making any facture propositionally redundant, as the conceptual artist Lawrence Weiner explicitly claims. The issue in all these works is the question, *What role must human agency have in relation to the creation of the art for it to be immediately acceptable as art?* Weiner's comments are typical of the devaluation of the physical object in favor of the same focus on artistic ideation (design) that appears in LeWitt's comments as well:

1. The artist may construct the piece.

2. The piece may be fabricated.

3. The piece need not be built.

Each being equal and consistent with the intent of the artist, the decision as to condition rests with the received upon the occasion of receivership. [...]

As to construction, please remember that as stated above there is no correct way to construct the piece as there is no incorrect way to construct it. If the piece is built it constitutes not how the piece looks but only how it could look.[82]

The object is irrelevant. Anything physical that could be produced following Weiner's conceptual work is, in a very basic sense, unimportant. In this model posed by *Conceptual Art* and software equally, the commodity expresses the self-actualization of reflective judgment (design) as the ideology of "autonomous achievement." The emphasis on the artist as the creator of the design in this schema— the selection and dictation of what the rules are—reifies the formal organization of production as the only significant act, rather than the outcomes of production created by labor. It anticipates the displacement of human labor in automation and the role of AI in performing the material production for the artist, per their instructions.

Sol LeWitt proposes answers to the question of human agency and its role by focusing on the initial design of the work, a concern with reflective judgments typical of *Conceptual Art* generally, that demonstrates how the class associations for intellectual labor denigrate determinative judgment—the productive action that "repeats past results" does so by applying an existing rule in directing agency. These are the same general developments that art historians Lucy Lippard and John Chandler discuss in their 1968 article "The Dematerialization of Art," which explains the shift both LeWitt and Weiner propose as a function of artists embracing the same managerial approach employed in the industrial factory:

> During the 1960s the anti-intellectual, emotional intuitive process of art-making characteristic of the [1940s and 1950s] have begun to give way to an ultra-conceptual art that emphasizes the thinking process almost exclusively. As more and more work is designed in the studio, but executed elsewhere by professional craftsmen, as the object becomes merely the end product, a number of artists are losing interest in the physical evolution of the work of art.[83]

The working process Lippard and Chandler describe precisely matches the regimentation of intellectual labor (design) versus physical facture (labor) as different and incompatible types of activity associated with distinct forms of judgment. The aesthetic production of *Conceptual Art* thus stands as the mirror image to *Pop Art*; both art movements are 'fellow travellers' embracing the dominant ideology of industrial capitalism in the 1960s. This belief in "autonomous achievement" elevates Kant's reflective judgment that chooses and creates (the expression of "genius") as an entirely different variety of agency from the labor required to implement those decisions. This approach to post-labor valorization pioneered in art is inherent in the rejection of human labor in digital capitalism—it reifies reflective judgment while dismissing determinative judgments as entirely irrelevant to the creation of the art. Reflective judgment enables the artist to "simply create" by employing skilled professional labor or an autonomous tool (their role is interchangeable) to perform the actual work of fabrication.

Conceptual Art thus parallels the invention of computer software: both express the societal hierarchy that enforces class differences between "artist" and "professional craftsman" as functions of prestige and value reflected in the different exchange values realized by their labor. The reflective judgment elevated by the Enlightenment ideal of rationality is the originary creative act of "genius" that produces *sui generis*; such an understanding is the humanist vision of "artist" as a special individual whose work is a product of personal sensitivities reflecting individual brilliance.[84] The human agency that designs the production of AI is what matters; the object itself being simply the result of those instructions, a "proof of function." Emphasizing the role of human agency in reflective judgment, rather than in the determinate application that is facture itself, affirms the cultural and material separation of managerial agency from labor. AI and automation do not challenge these distinctions, they convert them into instrumentalities.

These differences are implicit in Kant's comments on the separation between the superficial and the substance of art that will become by the mid-twentieth century the aesthetics of Formalist Modernism ably articulated by art critic Clement Greenberg:

> In painting, in sculpture, indeed in all the visual arts,
> including architecture and horticulture in so far are they are
> fine arts, *design* is what is essential; in design the basis for
> any involvement of taste is not what gratifies us in sensation,
> but merely what we like because of its form. The colors that
> illuminate the outline belong to charm. Though they can
> indeed make the object itself vivid to sense, they cannot
> make it beautiful and worthy of being beheld.[85]

Kant describes a transcendent evaluation concerned with bracketing the immanent experience from its relationship to an eternal, immaterial order that is only manifested to the mind; it is the duality between a realism of mere appearances and one of essences disclosed only to reason, the separation of mind and body. This dualism matches the division of judgments into the opposed categories of reflective (mind/management) and determinative (body/labor). These aesthetic valuations are exemplars for a transcendental ideological apparatus that directs attention away from the physical to an absent, imaginary order affirmed solely through intellectual activity. In industrialization it becomes the literal distinction between the designs used in the factory and their execution. This ideology appears in digital capitalism as both the aura of the digital that erases the physical from concern, and the aspiration to instrumentalize the state of information to render an immaterial physicality. It is an ideology concerned with denials of physical limits and restrictions that necessarily justify the cultural denigration of human labor in determinative judgment and devalue the practical exercise of agency.

§ 2.2.1 The Cultural Disenfranchisement
of Determinative Judgment

AI and autonomous agency, far more than the emergence of digital automation, challenges the established social order that developed around the valorization of human agency begun during the Enlightenment. The externalization of productive capacity as a commodity in capitalism is also a cultural and economic expression of the autonomy of human reasoning posited during the Enlightenment that is vested in reflective judgment; Kant's divisions of judgments into determinative and reflective mark different roles for human action in relation to facture as expressions of a resilient cultural order implicated in the capitalist demand for increased profits. The ideology of "autonomous achievement" denies the agency of determinative labor, a rejection that finds literal application in AI performing tasks that formerly required human intelligence. This cultural dislocation of labor in digital capitalism is a shift from its historically central role in production to becoming a continuous and contingent precariat where labor is conceived as a parasite—a Romantic extreme that rejects all social relationships and the virtues of compassion, empathy, and respect for others is inherent to this view, clearly expressed by Ayn Rand in the novel *Atlas Shrugged* via the character "John Galt":

> When need is the standard, every man is both a victim and a parasite. As a victim, he must labor to fill the needs of others, leaving himself in the position of a parasite whose needs must be filled by others. He cannot approach his fellow man except in one of two disgraceful roles: he is both a beggar and a sucker.[86]

The simplicity of this binary opposition posited by Rand illustrates the ideology of "autonomous achievement" as an idealized Rousseauian fantasy of self-sufficiency that is simultaneously solipsistic and nihilistic: hostile to the idea of any collective good or mutually beneficial activity, her ideology makes reciprocal exchange impossible, and denies the egalitarian culture of democracy by justifying the predatory nature of a social Darwinism in service to capitalist expansion. She promotes a fantasy that pretends the material infrastructure, political apparatus, and security arrangements that make capitalism possible are not a product of social relationships that require protection and maintenance, but an inevitable state of nature. Hers is a demand for entitlement without obligation. The differential value of reflective and determinative judgment appears in this binary opposition as an absolute split between the directive agency of management and the instructed agency of labor. It makes her rejection of social relationships a paradoxical assertion of Schumpeter's statement about the societal hierarchy "that those who cannot climb by these ladders [of success] are not worth troubling about."[87] The argument that equality is impossible because human beings are not equal in intelligence or success descends from this ideology. Enlightenment ideation around human agency becomes the internalized, literal substance of social differentiation in those societies *modernized* by industrialization; it is the feature that defines Modernity itself. The invention of AI is a product of this structural conflict over wages::profits that her comments assume as the only possible ordering of the societal hierarchy—an idealized, perfect capitalist competition in a marketplace without structural limits or barriers.[88]

Autonomous agency further diminishes the need for human intelligence in performing the determinative judgments of facture, by conversely elevating the already essential role of reflective judgments (design) by conceiving the autonomy of labor as a loss of control for management; capitalism realizes this denigration and disenfranchisement as the instrumentality of Taylorist scientific management. The Enlightenment demand for rationality becomes a structural contradiction between the different roles of agency in capitalism—direction and directed activity—that emerges dramatically with autonomous agency. As the decision process asserted by LeWitt's commentary on artistic production, this cultural division matches industrial rationalization and the ideological demonization of the 'degrees of freedom' afforded to labor in choosing how to proceed with production. The relative differences in wages of the CEO versus the janitor demonstrates this historical separation of roles—distinctions in wages that become comprehensible as an expression of the societal hierarchy—a demarcation of different cultural importance for reflective and determinative judgments, between those whose labor is considered culturally significant and those whose labor is not. The ongoing rental exerted by the *de facto* control system of DRM and the *de jure* systems of copyrights, patents, and trademarks are reciprocal methods for valorizing the principle of "first work" that is the reflective judgment.

§ 2.2.2 The Contradiction of Productivity and Exchange

Weak or stong, AI presents social and cultural challenges that are unlike the demands of work within the strictures of the factory that emphasized humans performing determinate, fixed actions without conscious reflection. As Marx noted, this denial of human agency thus renders human labor as part of the machine. Workers themselves are cast merely as the "intellectual organs"[89] within a regimented process. The elimination of the need for human labor to perform repetitive, rules–defined tasks with a limited range of determinate outcomes has several direct impacts on the cultural role of human agency:

[1] Human labor shifts to design (reflective judgment) in an expansion of the historically managerial role of directing/ overseeing the productive action of facture.

[2] AI creates new potentials for individual productivity that have historically been limited or restricted by the nature of productive labor and the costs associated with technical processes requiring not just labor, but highly skilled, specialized labor that becomes commonplace with digital automation.

[3] The society hierarchy that expresses cultural valuations through the division of managerial agency (intellectual labor) from that of labor (physical production) enters a crisis where AI threatens the essential difference that defines position within society.

The social order of this potential post-labor economy is a minimization and replacement of intelligent human labor (determinative judgment) by algorithmic systems. It succeeds precisely because the meaning of the activity being automated can be separated from its formal protocol. However, in eliminating the need for this type of human activity, every AI undermines the social distinctions and cultural hierarchies constructed around the incompatible demands in capitalism for profit and the necessity of its support for the social that allows profits to exist: the invention of autonomous agency undermines the integrity of capitalist valorization itself by restricting profit generation. Shifting the variable costs of social reproduction linked to human labor into the fixed costs of machinery is an attempt to resolve the diminishing rate of profit—yet it also denies the social necessity to support living labor that makes exchange possible. The devaluation of autonomous production is not sufficient to counteract this erosion of the social.

Digital capitalism, following the aura of the digital, reconceives wages as lost profits—but cannot resolve the imbalance it creates because it cannot remove human agency from the generation of profits, only minimize its role in commodity production. In a post-labor economy what necessarily remains as 'variable capital' is the minimized, but essential labor of management (production), while the human consumption of commodities (demand) that sets the machinery in motion needs to be maximized to generate profits (exchange). This contradiction between production and exchange is masked by ideology: the rate of profit may increase with AI, but the capacity to create exchange necessarily decreases—as does the value of the commodities generated by the autonomous system. In reducing the productive labor costs toward zero, it also reduces the commodity value by the same amount, a reciprocal relationship hidden by cultural beliefs that continue to support established rates of exchange and the societal hierarchy erected around them during industrialization.

§ 2.3 The Automation of Artistic Creation

The economic appeal of automation and AI as a corrective to the inherent vagaries of control, and to the ever-increasing costs of living labor is obvious: eliminating all non-managerial intelligent agency from production is a fantasy that converges on the same erasure of physicality described by the aura of the digital; it is the Enlightenment and Romantic belief in the creative "genius" unbounded by the material restrictions of skill, cost, and labor. These historical beliefs were sarcastically summoned by *New York Times* art critic Stuart Preston when confronted by the first exhibition of computer art in 1965:

> [Some day] almost any kind of painting can be computer-generated. From then on all will be entrusted to the '*deus ex machina*.' Freed from the tedium of techniques and the mechanics of picture making, the artist will simply create.[90]

His prediction about computers and art had come true by the 1990s. Digital systems have completely replaced the tedium of techniques and mechanics of picture making for some types of art production such as animation: the act of "rendering" what has been created in the virtuality of software is precisely a surrendering of facture to the automated processes Preston describes. For example, making an animated film in the Hollywood studios of the 1930s required an entire crew of human labor each performing a compartmentalized task. Oversimplifying this process still makes the volume of work to perform and the years of training and expertise required evident. The director oversees the process, but the actual animation is an assembly line process: the "tweeners" make each drawing between key poses provided by the director; "inkers" transfer these pencil drawings to acetate cells; "painters" fill in the colors—all tasks that had to be performed *before* photographing the film that would be shown in theaters. The complexity of synchronizing either the animated movements on-screen (as in lip-sync, for example) or the editing of the shots with a soundtrack only expands the complexity of this schematic process by adding additional layers of work to be performed. Additional complexity means additional labor. Contemporary 3D animation software now automates so much of this work that the entire animation pipeline can be performed by a child working alone at home, and the digital tools at their disposal can make highly polished results indistinguishable from work done at a commercial studio. This force magnifier does not eliminate the need for human agency, but does radically alter its role in the production process by emphasizing reflective judgment (design) in a literalization of LeWitt's proposals in *Sentences on Conceptual Art*.

The developments leading to this shift to "simply create" are unmistakable in proposals about the new art of software that emerged in the 1960s.[91] *Bell Labs* computer scientist A. Michael Noll identified the central role of human conception—an emphasis on agency rather than action—that converges with the isomorphism of ideation and execution in *Conceptual Art*.[92] By emphasizing human agency in directing the actions of digital automation, Noll casts the artist in the role of capitalist directing labor in the factory. Computers make the transfer of design into realization a direct implementation by eliminating the interference and interpretive mediation of human labor, as Noll explains:

> The creative process takes place in the mind of the artist; the final painting is only the artist's rendition of his mental image.[93]

The early computer art that Preston reviewed by artist-engineers such as Noll was concerned with the development and improvement of new tools—it was as much an invention of software for digital computer technology as a series of artifacts made by machines. In this model of facture, the human agency involved in deciding the actions to perform—programming the software (the instructions)—determines the art, is the art.[94] This separation of semiotic production from industrial production becomes important as the valorization of agency evolves, and consequently, in the capacity of digital capitalism to realize exchange around the commodity produced with automation. The creative act that strong AI specifically makes possible is both an expansion of control over the machinery of production and an elevation of the directive agency of management. Automation makes the ability of artists to "simply create" without concern for the costs of their work a logical reflection of a basic alteration in the nature of digital facture and the role of human agency in that process, since the shift to autonomous production is also a cultural denial of the physical costs imposed by time, skill, and the managerial role of human labor. This approach was summarized by author Steven Levy as a set of utopian principles he termed the "hacker ethic" that articulates the aura of the digital: all information should be free; mistrust authority—promote decentralization; hackers should be judged by their hacking, not criteria such as age, degrees, race or position; software is an art form; computers can change life for the better.[95] His utopian understanding of computers masks an ideology that views human labor as an interference in the 'true' agency of the managerial capitalist who directs the actions of labor through their designs. Even before the invention of AI, the role of labor in this process was irrelevant, relegated to the passive function of intelligent actions contained and ruled over by the agency that sets the system in motion, but with the emergence of AI, digital facture, and automated production the role of human agency undergoes a fundamental shift away from industrial production; the role of managerial agency (design) for these machinic operations makes how this structural change constrains production obvious. The assembly line was premised on the interchangeability of one commodity with another created in series as exemplars of a general type, such as sheets of paper in a ream of 500 where each sheaf is equally as good as another. With computer technology rendering a uniform quality of production not only commonplace, but exigent, the differentials between productions—aesthetics apparent as skill, quality, character—return as dominant features for valorization in the difference between the animation created in a commercial studio and that made by a child in their classroom. The undifferentiated nature of historical industrial production becomes immanent, on-demand bespoke facture.

§ 2.4 Futurity and Post-Labor

When human agency is not the vehicle of production, but its activator, valorization necessarily changes. This shift defines the essential parameter of the post-labor economy. It is a displacement of stored past production in favor of a proximate generative production that responds to the immediate request: the speed of delivery by companies such as *Amazon* is a response to the general immediacy of digital production, but applied to the distribution of material goods. It facilitates the illusion of surplussage created by on-demand production, like the output of the desktop printer, that is temporary, fleeting, and impermanent. This disposability is more than the planned obsolescence of the past; it is an effacement of commodity production conceived as a store of value. Instead, it reflects the shift to a currency based in futurity—the capacity to call production into existence—where commodity values are obligations reified as currency rather than past production identified by a receipt. The development of AI, autonomous agency, and the use of machine learning to perform complex, intelligent tasks promises an epochal shift in the nature of human society. The mobilization of past production via the "sharing economy" and its implementation through AI is a liquidation of past production that allows the extraction of these stored values and their consolidation by corporate power, an extractive action that mirrors the rental of software.

Replacing rote productive action with machinery is a cultural change even more than an economic one. The dismissal of the "lower" classes enacted by their replacement with machinery contradicts the earlier transition to industrialization and its makeover as post-Fordist knowledge work. Their role in society did not change with these earlier shifts. Their role in feudalism remained constant with industrialization, just as in the shift from industrialization to intellectual labor, but with the post-labor economy they are redundant: both weak and strong AI undermine the hierarchical distinction between lords and serfs that was retained in industrialization as the separation of management and labor.

The futurity of currency makes managerial agency into the operative demand for production rendered as a token of exchange. It is an obligation to perform labor, which in the post-labor economy means the capacity to order AI into operation. This valorization of the reflective judgment (design) that is the *causa sui* of facture is a shift in power relations that is premised on the restrictive control of DRM: only those with the right to demand production can receive it. This valorization of those aristocratic prerogatives of reflective judgment formerly only associated with the dominant classes in society becomes the primary mechanism of commodity creation and exchange. The formal restrictions of asymmetrical power enshrined in patent law, copyright, and DRM, as well as the consolidation of intellectual property and the commodification of human social action are all attempts to maintain the established order and societal hierarchy as the cultural foundations of industrial society metamorphose into a new configuration, the 'society of leisure,' whose utopian aspiration is a society where the familiar class distinctions have melted into air.

§ 3. USE LIMITS VALUE

Historical industrial capitalism obscures a foundational constraint on autonomous value generation: the social demand for *utility*. The requirement for a commodity to meet a human need or desire, evident in the act of exchange. This factor limits the valorization of semiotic production by AI systems and their replacement of human agency.[96] Use appears to be an entirely separate concern from economic relations only because it motivates the exchange process, preceding it: without use, no exchange occurs, making it the essential social and cultural restraint, and a precondition to valorization. The historical refusal in capitalism to consider this antecedent to exchange leads to the mutually contradictory fantasies of the aura of the digital in the proposal that AI will inaugurate a new golden age of prosperity and wealth-without-labor, and its opposite, a dystopian future of humanity enslaved, destitute, and unemployed by the machinery that rendered human agency obsolete. Both fantasies deny physicality to imagine all production without human labor as intrinsically and equally valuable, but what is being ignored in this claim is the common role of human agency in production and in exchange. The term for this other dimension, "utilization," identifies a parallel process to valorization; utility is not limited to the designed functionality of a commodity, but instead depends on the metaphysical relationships of social and cultural significance.[97] Use mobilizes social interaction, and its central productive role as the subject of pervasive monitoring (surveillance) acknowledges its necessity by acting as a mechanism for gauging demand from observations of the social functions that exist. The manipulations of "public relations" (and the engineered irrational of agnotology) implement this information in an attempt to create interest and demand for specific commodities.[98] Agnotology::surveillance used in marketing describes socio–cultural factors that devolve to use, as Noll explained about *AT&T's* attempts to introduce the picturephone in the 1960s following its popular demonstration at the 1964 *New York World's Fair*:

> Technology is only successful if it satisfies the actual needs of real consumers. Decades ago, *AT&T* discovered that all the promotion in the world could not convince most people

that they needed a *picturephone*. Technology offers—but consumers decide.[99]

The social acceptance identified by the use for a commodity determines both proximate demand and its potential for exchange: with physical facture this requirement for utility provides an instantly clear limit on all production, since anything without a complementary use becomes "waste," lost capital. The example of *AT&T's* failed *picturephone* is an instance of this social restriction where the capitalist demand for surplus value (profit) intersects with use to reduce and prevent waste.[100] This historical requirement affirms the basic social restriction on excessive waste; however, the force magnifier of both weak and strong AI reduces labor costs via database manipulation leveraged by machine learning to generate potential values without limits, producing a useless commodity that digital capitalism nevertheless seeks to realize as/into value. This production–without–use brings the inherent restriction on valorization—*utilization*—into consciousness as an impediment to the exchange process. These constraints are revelations of how the historical mismatches between costs of production (facture) and the necessity for use (demand) articulate a pair of linked assumptions within capitalist production that all AI renders moot:

[1] All production is an answer to some proximate, defined need or use, whether as necessary subsistence or in a demonstration of social position.

[2] Labor costs constrain production in such a way that exchange value necessarily implies use value through the *causa sui* of social demand for production.[101]

Utilization is an emergent constraint on exchange value separate from concerns with labor (agency) and the material substance of the commodity (the object). An excessive accumulation of potential values without use is possible through the combination of on-demand facture and the semiotic recombination of the database by AI. The potential values derived from this generative activity illustrates the contradiction between [1] and [2], since historical capitalism assumes all commodity production is valuable even if it has not realized any value via exchange. The futurity of currency in digital capitalism, much like these immaterial potential commodities, upends these assumptions about value reified in production: it is the human demand that is valuable for the post-labor economy, an issue of utilization rather than production. The immaterialism that defines digital capitalism is about the extractive profits created by the processes of being sold or marketed, as Giles Deleuze noted in the 1990s.[102] This transitional shift to an immaterial churn of semiotic processes shows the change from an economic of material production to one of contingent demand that enables valorization. The great stock market valuation of *Facebook* or *Google* reflects their capacity to provoke and manipulate these essential human demands; this control is the source of their value, derived from the databases of highly valuable user data they have built through pervasive monitoring.

Human validation of a commodity through utilization provides the substance of the database generated directly by pervasive monitoring, as well as indirectly through human agency authorizing facture (demand). The reciprocity of these twin factors creates a cycle of self-reinforcing pervasive monitoring. Even when the digital system is entirely autonomous, the initiation of the performed task relies on human agency via demand—especially when the role for that agency is highly truncated. An autonomous vehicle can perform a complex series of actions in driving from one location to another without proximate oversight, yet those actions are always responding to human demands. Human agency is central—the self-driving car does not go to a shopping mall's parking lot on its own and decide that it is a nice place to 'hang out.' This parasitic dependence on human agency does not alter the autonomy of the system any less than human labor performing a task without continuous oversight. The initiating agency remains dominant, an expression of the demand that sets every AI in motion—the *prima causa* that employs autonomous labor is always human. All machine operations ultimately descend from a human demand or instruction that activates the device: surplus value necessarily devolves from utility realized via exchange. It is a process that creates two antithetical varieties: the first is the cycle of wages::profits; the second is the extractive transfer of wealth that removes it from this cycle. These dynamics are expressions of how the social organizes value and distributes production. Acknowledging that when exchange does not match a complementary human wage returning the surplus to circulation within the economy the profits created by production without human labor necessarily adopt the appearance of being–magical since the values it offers seem to appear *sui generis*: the surplus value created by weak and strong AI appears to arise as a profit-without-expenditure—an illusion produced by the aura of the digital's effacing of physical costs and constraints from consideration that allows a purely extractive profit taking to happen invisibly. This looting of existing values is made possible because the costs of AI, like the fixed costs of resources and material consumed in production, are masked by the force magnification of machinery that counteracts the continuous decline in the rate of profit by transforming variable labor costs into fixed costs, a savings that superficially mirrors the extraction it creates. The social response to these lacunae, the taxation of profits generated by AI, appears to be an inevitable mechanism to reclaim this extractive value that creates the scarcity of capital.[103]

Utility is fundamentally an ethical assessment expressed via exchange that stands apart from the issue of value justifying expenditures consumed in facture. Social demands for use act as a limit and control on the productive capacity of automation because resources are always limited. The aura of the digital denies these constraints inherited from historical infopoor societies that restricted commodity production automatically by its difficulty and resource consumption. Semiotic facture by any AI system uses the same solution, manipulating the database, as a corrective to limitations on valorization in the inforich society of digital capitalism: this "unfinite" archive becomes apparent in the universal preservation of all data—it is a commodity whose value is proportional to the scale of potential value it contains (size and complexity of the database). However expansive this virtual resource may be, the physical limits on commodity production become apparent once the issue of expenditure is considered as a function of scarcity and the difficulty of all facture. In infopoor societies where value was determined over time as wholly a function of utility only those things with functional application were produced or preserved. Thus "waste" employed in demonstrations of social status in infopoor societies assumes a specific valence as expressions of leisure—that the "waste" can be safely accepted without consequence.[104] These factors have been obscured by the successive waves of industrial production: increased efficiencies have enabled the aura of the digital and its fantasy of continuous growth and infinite profit without physical restriction.

In digital capitalism the historical limits of utility in the infopoor society have been denied and ignored because they are a reflection of *necessary* production constraining its consumption and thereby limiting the potential for surplus value generation. Utility restricts the autonomous value of contemporary inforich society, mirroring the restrictions imposed by the material costs of historical production. Potential values generated by autonomous processing devolve upon specific human demands and ultimately require human action to realize any value via exchange. Valorization and wealth in the post-labor economy depends on this pathology emergent in the mismatch of demand and potential value. The necessity of utilization reflects how production costs are radically truncated by the speed and efficiency of AI; when there are no costs for creating potential value, there are few restrictions on its generation, making utility even more central to controlling this profligate generation.

The ethical questions that utilization poses about the type, necessity, and impacts of facture have been consistently ignored in the capitalist demand for continuous, infinite growth. The role of the social in this realization of potential values demonstrates the centrality of human relationships. The immaterial standing reserve awaiting human demand does not consume resources in the same manner that physical production always does—the immaterial surplus becomes immanent value–without–use (following the aspiration to the state of information), a by-product of on-demand digital facture. Utility becomes *the* limit and determinant of value for immaterial facture in the 'society of leisure'—especially apparent in digital distribution, and immanent "on demand" production using 3D printers. The harms caused by these centuries-old capitalist expansions of profit-taking have always been immanent in the environmental destruction, social oppression, human misery, poverty, illness, and death created through the refusal to consider or include the ethical issues of commodity distribution or resource depletion in assessing the costs of capitalist production due to the elision of utilization and utility in its analysis—factors that return to the foreground in the post-labor economy.

§ 3.1 Contingent Demand

AI is a tool not only for the production of commodities, but also for the manipulation of human needs and desires via "public relations" in an attempt to transform potential values into profits by avoiding mismatches between production (utility), productive capacity (facture), and human desire (demand). As in all production, and explicit in the productive shift from physical manufacture to the immaterial semiosis characteristic of digital production, the creation of profit (surplus value) depends on the social relationships of labor, exchange, and utilization. Pervasive monitoring builds the databases that are central to the manipulation of human desires in digital capitalism, becoming apparent in the role of this mechanism in creating markets and demand for new production. This role for pervasive monitoring defines the creation of 'contingent demand' in the demographic analysis of audiences that "public relations" then translates into the creation of surplus value. This creation/management of human desire dovetails with the valorization of the data that enables its manipulation, making the data into a commodity in itself—thereby bridging the immaterial labor of organizing and selecting what is produced and the domain addressed by the individualized demographic study. This increasingly granular isolation of consumers as individuals reveals the hypothetical ideal of digital advertising in the singular 'market of one.' These dynamics constrain profit generation. They are especially apparent in the limiting role of human labor on production in the performing arts, as well as in art generally; the impacts of contingent demand becoming dominant in the creation of popular art concerns film director Martin Scorsese in a *The New York Times* op-ed:

> The [Marvel superhero films and other franchise] pictures
> are made to satisfy a specific set of demands, and they are

designed as variations on a finite number of themes. They are sequels in name but they are remakes in spirit, and everything in them is officially sanctioned because it can't really be any other way. That's the nature of modern film franchises: market-researched, audience-tested, vetted, modified, revetted and remodified until they're ready for consumption.[105]

The highly competitive marketplace created by a vastly expanded media environment that includes the traditional movie theater, cable, broadcast, and premium television, as well as the newer delivery systems that stream programs through the Internet on "channels" such as *Netflix*, *Disney+*, or *Amazon Prime Video* creates complex challenges that contingent demand attempts to mitigate. Scorsese notes this increased competition, stating:

It's a perilous time in film exhibition, and there are fewer independent theaters than ever. The equation has flipped and streaming has become the primary delivery system.[106]

His comments illustrate how historical productions valorized in markets with low competition had more capacity for deviation created by differences in talent and artistry than they do in the contemporary highly competitive marketplace that leaves fewer options for less-than-ideal success.[107] The response being adopted—bigger budgets, more sex, violence, and spectacle—accompanies a more carefully managed production to link the contents of the work to the interests of its audience. Demographic modeling employed in the Marvel superhero films and other franchise pictures is an attempt to attract larger audiences and maintain the rate of profit. These constraints reduce the variety of what is shown in movie theaters in an attempt to maximize profits on each production. Contingent demand is this careful and continuous adjustment to maximize market response in an attempt to manage and create audiences that impacts both the marketing and the production itself. AI is central to this process. It instrumentalizes the demographic data provided by the focus groups and market research which Scorsese describes; the system of pervasive monitoring that supports these manipulations is an application of the marketing common to "public relations," but is also a product of that marketing. The cultural impact is the creation of a "winner take all" marketplace, with its accompanying limitation to works that reflect and support the dominant *status quo*.

Simultaneously, the new technologies developed for reduced cost, greater control, and increased efficiency serve to liberate production from the historically familiar controls and constraints. The historical assumption that motion pictures were not an everyday production, generally available to the public is simply no longer valid, an expansion of production mirroring how automation enables new forms of creative work without requiring the same historical apparatus. This shift is a symptom-effect of the technological shift Scorsese notes that is rendering the process of *production–distribution–consumption* as the commodity, rather than the completed film. Both the rental of software via a subscription model and the "hosting" of media-delivery systems such as *YouTube* or *Vimeo* as a commodity/service demonstrate a valorization of media production/consumption. The automated editorial presentation of media within these "open" and democratic systems makes the importance of cultural authority more evident. The Post-Modern crisis of cultural authority that critic Craig Owens described in 1983 as an embrace of alternatives and ambivalence[108] that anticipates the fragmentation and decentering accompanying the rise of the digital no longer describes the Contemporary:

> Decentered, allegorical, schizophrenic [...] however we
> choose to diagnose its symptoms, Post-Modernism is usually
> treated, by its protagonists and antagonists alike, as a crisis
> of cultural authority, specifically of the authority vested in
> Western European culture and its institutions. [... 'But
> perhaps the most eloquent testimony to the end of Western
> sovereignty has been that of Paul Ricoeur, who wrote in 1962
> that "the discovery of the plurality of cultures is never a
> harmless experience."[109]

Owens' description of Post-Modernism as a "crisis of cultural authority" is a natural consequence of the leveling of hierarchies and democratic expansion. Yet, it does not render those authorities moot. Instead, the plurality of additional voices that were initially destabilizing rapidly became an expansion in/of markets as "globalization," offering new opportunities for valorization and capitalist colonization. His Post-Modern crisis of cultural authority is now over; however, a new, cultural crisis of social status is only just beginning. Access, recognition, and acknowledgment are limited, social resources. The role of existing institutions in administering cultural authority increases as a mechanism to manage the social disruptions posed by the democratic expansions in *production–distribution–consumption* most evident with AI. Scorsese's objections to the "franchise pictures" is a reflection of these conflicts over the social functions of cultural authority in this period of transition.

The plurality of additional voices ironically reinforces the traditional social dominance of institutions and their administration of status. For the mass marketed commodities that are commercial motion pictures—both the "franchise pictures" and Scorsese's own work—the gate keeping provided by the film studios and their control over production and exhibition is a mechanism of social status. The democratic expansion created by digital tools entails a shift of the means of production into being a commodity, thus modeling the "vanity press": where the manufacturing is the commodity, rather than what is produced. At the same time, fragmented markets makes the publicity and marketing that have always been an essential part of all performing arts, whether cinematic or otherwise even more important. AI makes this highly detailed management of demand more effective. The role of marketing and demographics in the production of motion pictures is not new—it is a common feature of the entire history of the Hollywood system in the United States. Audience demands constrain these commercial media productions, affirming the central role of the demographic constraints on production that are the focus of Scorsese's objections. The emergence of automation in demographic analysis enables a new attempt to 'solve' to the falling rate of profit: the creation of performance-commodities that "perfectly" match the contingent demands of their particular audiences, ensuring their marketability to those audiences. This dominance of market research and audience testing in contemporary cinema is an acknowledgement of value as a social relationship dependent on human interests and desires that must be mobilized to create audiences: either a broad, general audience (as Scorsese describes), or a narrowing of these considerations to realize an ideal, hypothetical 'market of one' offered by the targeted advertising of social media. The cultural demand that realizes surplus value for art demonstrates the centrality of social and aesthetic concerns in the creation and maintenance of audiences, since those who agree with Scorsese's critique would not be likely to attend showings of the franchise films he describes. The equal capacity of weak and strong AI to sort data and provide results allows a tailoring of production to precisely match audience demands is an attempt to maintain profits by creating cinematic work that matches the audience's expectations as entertainment, distraction, and spectacle.

§ 3.2 Baumol's Cost Disease

Concerns with values generated by "return on investment" (ROI) suggest the common concern with translating utility (use value) into profit from expenditure;[110] however, this utility is superficial, as ROI is immanent in nature, demanding an immediate delivery (the "return" or profit). The centrality of this concern is the implicit object of Scorsese's critique, a complaint about "quality" based in the idea of *l'art pour l'art*—that aesthetics and artistic pursuits should be independent of their use or exchange values. The issue of profit for the shift from valorizing determinative judgment (labor) to valorizing reflective judgment (design) is apparent in the parallax between creative thought and the performing arts, parallel tendencies whose differences make the limitations of automation as a replacement for the intellectual labor of reflective judgment apparent. The issue of wages::profits is the question of ROI that dominates in aesthetic productions: ROI for the arts is a shift to concerns with immediate profit generation. Rather than demonstrating a concern with use, it masks the liquidation of production in the performance—once performed, the labor is expended but the commodity has also been consumed; the commodity is the labor itself. Media such as motion pictures and sound recordings avoid this self-destructing character of performance, but only partly. Scorsese's critique describes the use of agnotology::surveillance in an attempt to avoid the singular and inalterable unity of artistic works that limits their utilization. This failing is Baumol's "cost disease," where greater hours of artistic labor do not produce greater commodity value, and the costs of production remain resolutely fixed, incommensurate with the functions of AI and automation in reducing the costs of design for artistic creation:

> The performer's labors themselves constitute the end product which the audience purchases. Any change in the training and skill of the performer or the amount of time he spends before the audience affects the nature of the service he supplies. [...] The immediate result of this technological difference between live performance and the typical manufacturing industry is that while productivity is very much subject to change in the latter [manufacturing], it is relatively immutable in the former [performance].[111]

There is no change in the labor time required to produce artistic works, even though the procedural labor of facture for media such as animation can be automated. The labor required in a performance of play lasting two hours will always be the same two hours of labor, a denial of both efficiency and productivity gains in other types of facture.[112] Baumol's analysis of economic problems surrounding the performing arts also applies to all the other arts: while it is not concerned with motion pictures, the same problematics of value and labor impact both its exhibition and the performance work that creates/is the film. The entanglement of ROI and marketing with the constraints of contingent demand that Scorsese decries arises from the financial stress of the mounting operating deficits in production/marketing common to all performing arts. There can be no substitution of lower cost, lesser skilled labor without creating dramatic and unanticipated changes to the quality of the aesthetic work produced that directly impact its value as a commodity. A painting by Theo van Gogh is not a substitute nor an equivalent for one by his brother, Vincent van Gogh. The process of production and valorization for the arts appears to be resistant to the forces of automation and AI, denying the equivalence that is the foundation of rationalized production on the assembly line. The incommutability between an aesthetic work by one artist and a lesser work by another (or even a greater and lesser work by the same artist) is what leads to the dramatic concerns with giving the audience what they want to see that Scorsese describes as anti-cinematic. The coming–into–dominance of contingent demand to ensure ROI is a palliative for increased competition, symptomatic of failed attempts to reverse the increasing costs of production and the expanded competition for audiences described in Baumol's analysis of the performing arts.

AI has become essential to the contingent demand that Scorsese describes via the perception of utility—achieved through the process of being "market-researched, audience-tested, vetted, modified, revetted and remodified" that attempts to precisely match the product to the audience's desires for it. For 'fixed' media, once the piece has been created it becomes a material asset, subject to the same exchange and valorization as other commodities, but the costs of its creation lie in the vagaries of live performance, rather than assembly line production, a model of production that anticipates the individuation of the post-labor economy with its atomized 'audience of one.' The incipient 'society of leisure' describes a cultural order where the autonomous, on-demand production of all AI corresponds with the human desires that set it in motion—a personalized production that is historically categorically different from that of industrial assembly lines. Elements of this contingency inform the automated delivery of advertising online: informed by pervasive monitoring, the ads delivered are matched to assessments generated by AI that identify personal desires and link them to the products offered.

§ 3.4 Autonomous Artistry

While the capacity to automate the performances of actors in cinema is emerging with the various photo-realistic puppeting tools, that are most dramatically evident in the phenomenon of AI generated "deep fakes" that alter footage in one motion picture to simulate the use of different actors, these developments are accentuations of the same automation already in use for animation that still relies on the directorial control of reflective judgment—the performative artistic creation whose cost problems Baumol theorizes. Digital technologies and automation in cinema are examples of commercial demands for lower cost, increased control, and greater efficiency in all phases of pre-production, production, and post-production. Critic Steven Shaviro has described this transformation of historically rare and marginal techniques that manipulate live action according to the priorities of animation/VFX into a commonplace part of media as "post-cinema," a reflection of the impact that digital automation has on established cinematic aesthetics:

> Everything can be sampled, captured, and transcribed into a string of ones and zeroes. This string can then be manipulated and transformed, in various measures and controllable ways. Under such conditions, multiple differences ramify endlessly; but none of these differences actually *makes a difference*, since they are all completely interchangeable.[113]

Shaviro's emphasis on digital transformations—the animation of the samples—is a concern with the "image–animation problem,"[114] a recognition that cinema depends on a fragmentation protocol which allows precise manipulations of screen contents as *sui generis* expressions unto themselves, disconnected from any profilmic reality or the ontological foundation assumed by the established cinema aesthetics of film theorist André Bazin and the French *Nouvelle Vague* of the 1960s whose theories Scorsese defends in his editorial.[115] Unlike the physical photograph-samples of historical film where each image is a complete fixed unit, digital imagery shown on-screen is assembled from discrete pixels that allow a robust individual manipulation.[116] However, for the audience, the historical and contemporary motion pictures rendered by these dissimilar processes equally hide their technological origins in the low-level, foundational perceptions that are denotation and movement;[117] instead, higher-level interpretations dominate—the "real content" that the audience is interested in seeing (the story).[118] The capacity to transform the image-content of cinema with digital technology transitions into the artificial generation of those contents in a seamless spectrum of developments. The role of AI and automation in this process offers the potential to eliminate the human performance required for these works: the creation of a fully autonomous spectacle generated for an idealized 'audience of one' would extend these developments to their logical conclusion. It is a solution to the problem of Baumol's cost disease connected to performance where the human labor in this creation vanishes entirely, leaving only the fixed costs of machinery and material—a parallel to the productive shift from physical manufacture to immaterial semiosis: using minimal expenditures to maximize profits for the arts are an attempt to efface the declining rate of profit shown by the equation **surplus/(constant capital+variable capital)**.

The historical role for automation in art production illuminates these dynamics. It replicates the use of skilled professional craftspeople in the fabrication of *Minimalist* sculpture and *Conceptual Art* in the

1960s, replacing human labor with machinery. Artist Roxy Paine's painting–making system, the *PMU* (*Painting Manufacture Unit*) is a labor–saving device created in 1999–2000. This computer controlled machine follows the artist's instructions to produce paintings with a spray nozzle that squirts white acrylic paint onto raw canvas. These 36–by–59 inch paintings approximate the 'golden section' familiar from classical art, but Paine's labor–saving device fabricates paintings that are anti-illusionistic. The action of producing the work becomes its subject—painterly contents directly evoking the flat, reflexive, and non-mimetic style of Formalist painting promoted by Clement Greenberg.[119] The *PMU* creates descendants of the poured paintings of Jackson Pollock or Morris Louis, while referencing the same use of raw canvas as in Willem de Kooning or Paul Cézanne's images. These are paintings that no human could (or would) paint by hand—they depend on a time consuming process that is onerous for human labor, but easily accomplished by automation. The results of this operation create paintings where the *paint* is literally sliding off the canvas, a material presentation that asserts the physicality of the image base and its gravitational relationship to the floor of the gallery.

However, in a reminder of Baumol's cost disease, the production time for one of these paintings created by the *PMU* remains constant: it is limited by the physical production time required for the paint to dry between successive coats. All the automation does is ratify this material limit as the foundational, minimum production time. The *PMU* is not even a weak AI, yet it identifies the same problems any AI creates: the costs of human labor are eliminated by the reduced costs of machinery; however, these costs are irrelevant to the *utilization* of artworks, which is connected directly to the questions of the societal hierarchy, cultural importance, and aesthetic traditions . . . these complex dynamics between the novelty of a work and its relationship to the schema 'art' aligns the generative products of Paine's *PMU* with the triumphant Modernist aesthetics of the mid-twentieth century.[120] The assumptive beliefs in originality and genius that were essential to aesthetic value at that time were articulated by American composer Harry Partch in 1949:

> Perhaps the most hallowed of traditions among artists of
> creative vigor is this: traditions in the creative arts are per se
> suspect. For they exist on the patrimony of standardization,
> which means degeneration. They dominate because they are
> to the interest of some group that has the power to perpetuate
> them, and they cease to dominate when some equally
> powerful group undertakes to bend them to a new pattern.[121]

Only those works that overturned traditions were important, thus ratifying reflective judgment as the only activity with cultural significance. These avant-garde challenges to established aesthetics via the innovative work of the genius artist who breaks the "weight of tradition" are central to the aesthetics of mid-century Modernist painting by artists such as Jackson Pollock, an aesthetic that is parodied by the mechanism of the *PMU*. The cultural importance of these aesthetic productions lies, in part, with how they have specifically internalized the disruptive impacts of new technology on art in the nineteenth century as a mechanism to avoid a deskilling of aesthetic production and maintain its value and role in the societal hierarchy. This impact is obvious with how the invention of photography "short-circuited" the technical skill required of painters: prior to its invention, high-quality portraiture was the exclusive domain of the elites, but the photograph allowed a democratic, general access to something that was previously rare, very expensive, and difficult to produce. By making what had been previously a class distinction available to everyone at a low price (eliminating the cost restriction that maintains that elite's access) photography disrupted art by imposing a form of cultural democracy that both weak and strong AI now have the potential to do for facture generally. The closed loop of *production–distribution–consumption* affirms this paradoxical standardization of bespoke facture by eliminating aberrant variations that offer the potential to change the dynamics in question. The internalization of this disruptive approach as the avant-garde's overturning and assault on expectations is now standard museal practice, a shift that art historian Renato Poggioli anticipated in 1946,[122] and philosopher of art, Arthur Danto identified in 1997 as having become the baseline condition of Contemporary art:

> In the sense that certain things were not possible for a
> European or an African in 1890, everything is possible today.
> Still we are locked into history. We cannot have the system of
> exclusionary beliefs that prevented artists in Europe from
> making masks and fetishes. We cannot be such a European
> for the same reason that such a European could not have
> been an African. But there are no forms today that are
> forbidden us. All that is forbidden us is that they should have
> the kind of meaning they had when they were forbidden us.
> But these are limitations well lost. It is no limit on the idea of
> freedom that we are not free to be prisoners![123]

The alienation created by the capture of human agency by pervasive monitoring instrumentalizes the "free" situation described by Danto.[124] It is easy to recognize Clement Greenberg's Modernist "formalism" within this description of the avant-garde becoming an academic procedure. This assimilation of the disruptive impacts inaugurated by photography that undermined the costs that made art too expensive, too difficult to manufacture, too restricted to an elite class has maintained the social function of art—its *use*—as a class differentiator; the expansions of art genres produced by the avant-garde since the mid-twentieth century has even become a new source of markets apparent how the Post-Modern and Contemporary includes those marginalized and neglected audiences and subject matter excluded in the Modernist aesthetics of the 1950s.[125] Both these expansions of audiences and the use of automation are symptoms of the structural need to address Baumol's cost disease—it is the same palliative process of simultaneously finding/guaranteeing markets and eliminating costs that defines the franchise motion picture. The necessity of utility (use) in this construction of ROI is merely a pretext for mechanics that allows an extraction of profit; it has no significance otherwise. The valorization of art makes the centrality of utility apparent in how the aesthetic, cultural and social uses of artworks matches those concerns common to historical conceptions of capitalism, but with a difference: these valorizations are disconnected from questions of labor and material, anticipating the productive emphases of the post-labor economy.[126] This change gives the valorization of art a convergence with the production–without–use typical of autonomous production.

These performative limits are cultural impacts of AI precisely because in the post-labor economy, the differences of artistry (design) are what determine the valorization and the capacity to generate surplus value. These historical difficulties posed by creating profit from artistic endeavors that were limited to live performances, and which apply to the recorded performances of motion pictures or music, as well as the generative performances common to the interactivity of video games expand in the post-labor economy to encompass the bespoke on-demand productions created for the 'audience of one.' The introduction of automation into the performative fabrication of aesthetic works corresponds to the same problem with the rate of profit that Baumol's cost disease identified; uniformity is the ultimate result of these attempts to address the maintenance of profits by attempting to guarantee their audience. The reduction and elimination of human labor in these productions matches the same replacement of human labor in the industrial factory; it is an attempt to resolve the costs of variable labor by replacing it with technology. The democratic dimensions of these expansions of audience are apparent in how the demographic construction discussed by Scorsese and the automatic simulation of photoreal animation are converging trends that imply a developmental goal to generate a media work specifically for a small or singular audience on-demand without the need for *any* human labor in its creation—an autonomously generated spectacle.

§ 3.4 Scarcity of Capital

The issue posed by weak or strong AI is not unemployment, nor even replacement, but of how every AI initially pretends to be a complementary filling–in of the short falls between productive capacity and available labor that maintains the immaterial values contained in/as titles to future production—the scarcity of capital formed by the number of obligations to initiate production expanding beyond the ability of production to meet those demands. The lack of capital in circulation within the economy that results in a cessation of production arising from the periodic, structural crises from excessive speculation, overproduction, or other mismatches between demand and production; every implementation of AI appears to provide a mechanism for both mediating shortfalls in production and managing contingent demand. At the same time, the digital appears to naturalize the concentration of capital that creates the scarcity of capital, since the digital itself poses as a magical resource that can be used without consumption or diminishment, leading to the fantasy of accumulation without production, the mythical "free lunch" countered by the values contained in the cycle of wages::profits generated from human agency. The post-labor economy posed AI is an extension of those developments begun in the late twentieth century as semiotic manipulation replaced the physical commodity form, and automated semiotic facture that created immaterial commodities replaced physical production. Both weak and strong AI equally bridge the gap between physical asset and virtual commodity, allowing their convergence to legitimate immateriality as a vehicle for wealth production. The emerging role of autonomous agency in facture is a symptom of a larger cultural shift from considerations and valuations based in physical processes towards potential values that are not subject to the limitations of physical production, only to the scarcity of capital the demand for utility, and the activation of facture by human desire.

The post-labor economy is fundamentally based in immaterialism—values created without productive human agency—a change that will generate highly disruptive social, cultural, political and economic impacts evident in the types of task that AI performs more quickly and more efficiently than any human labor can: those activates that involve complex yet rote actions, as for example in the recognition, identification and collation of personal information gained from surveillance. The high-speed matching of faces seen in the crowd, linked to their individual demographic data is a task that human labor struggles to complete at all, yet it is precisely the type of labor that weak AI is already performing. The existing valorization of agency in capitalism only conceives of this production as valuable in terms of the database it creates—the collection activity is incidental, even though it is the principle labor involved. The productive activity of AI has almost no economic value in itself. This discrepancy is indicative of how autonomous production is a mechanism subsumed into the valorization of the database: its extent, contents, and accessibility are what determine the commodity value. Restricting access is a precondition to valorize operations on the database; the "open" and "free" databases used for web search such as *Google, Baidu, Bing* or *DuckDuckGo* are different than those of social media that require personal identifiers to use, such as *Facebook*. Yet in all these cases, their "free" cost is a mechanism to facilitate data collection on their users that allows them to expand and enhance their actual profit-generating business—selling advertising through the combination of AI and pervasive monitoring. The values generated through this presentation of sales pitches are highly extractive since they are disproportionately mismatched to the labor involved in their creation.

What this distinction has to do with the problem posed by the scarcity of capital is simple: while AI appears to offer a solution to the mismatch between available labor and titles to future production (currency), it does not. The solution AI technology provides is illusory precisely because the labor provided by the machine is not the source of value; neither are the individual products of that labor—only their aggregate, such as the accumulation in a database, is valuable. The database is the essence of the determinative judgment since it is the actual product of both weak and strong AI systems. The scarcity of capital continually haunts these activities since "public relations" is a type of affective performance (thus subject to the same mismatch that Baumol's cost disease identifies) rather than productive. Autonomous agency brings the original distinction of capitalist valorization of agency into consciousness: the difference between managerial labor (conceived as reflective judgment) and the productive labor of facture (determinative judgment). The separation of these two "principal" elements described by Marx in *Capital* reflects the conversion of the emancipated agrarian serf who in becoming free must now sell their agency as a commodity in the city, and the emergent bourgeois who replaced the feudal lords, buying that agency and in the process replacing the aristocratic political structure with a new, mercantile one. The Enlightenment proposal of democracy is necessarily in opposition to this replication of the feudal order; in the industrial factory and digital capitalist office equally, the trade union mirrors this revenant segmentation of management (lords) versus labor (serfs), and the attacks on unionization in countries such as the United States demonstrate the incompatibility between the authoritarian order of capitalism and the egalitarian order created by the Enlightenment's concerns with agency. The economic dynamics of labor unions versus management are examples of these structural mismatches; the opposition between capitalism and the social is an inherent dimension of this societal organization. The forces within digital capitalism that oppose any democratic expansion create impediments to the emancipation of labor through the ideology of "autonomous achievement" and the "Protestant Work Ethic."

The scarcity of capital cannot be addressed by the autonomous agency of machines; it is a social product, emergent in the centrality of human labor to the creation of value and the incapacity for surplus value to emerge without the exchange relationship enabled by wages. To shift into a different system, such as one based in a stipend, grant, or entitlement such as "universal basic income" alters these historical relationships, creating new imbalances—but remains constrained by the limited capacity of production, whether performed by human labor or by an AI.

There can be no substitution of automation for the central factor of *human* productive capacity without fundamentally altering the existing social distribution of wealth (titles to initiate production). Automation does not change these existing imbalances, neither does it correct them: it only makes the inequalities and injustices more apparent and more directly a threat to the continued cycle of wages::profits that creates surplus value. In attempting to overcome the barrier wages prepresent for profit generation and erect a new barrier to the societal hierarchy being changed by AI, this process exacerbates the crisis, thereby accelerating the need for more changes, instead of maintaining the *status quo* by resolving them. The structural demands of capitalism encourage human actors to make certain decisions, but those choices are always the responsibility of the people who make them: the fiction of the corporation and capitalism in general is that capitalists are not responsible for their actions because the natural order (structural demand) makes them do it. It is a sectarian version of "the Devil made me do it." The deployment of AI to achieve any partial or even total displacement of human labor may not be in the service of an expansion of democracy, but is instead a mechanism to more permanently secure the unearned privileges attached to the ownership roles that dominate the societal hierarchy and are enshrined in the corporation.

Figure 4.1: Helena Glory (Frances Carson) questions the robot
Radius (Leslie Banks) in Act 2 of a performance of Karel Čapek's
play *Rossumovi Univerzální Roboti* (*Rossum's Universal Robots*) at
St. Martin's Theatre, London, England, 1923.

§ 4. ETHICAL AUTONOMY
AND HUMAN AGENCY

The transfer of human agency to the autonomous machine ratifies the state of information as a pure instrumentality. Weak and strong AI make the centrality of human agency apparent through their subservience to the human demands that put the machine in motion, because only humans are or can be responsible: first, the people who produce the machine are responsible for the laws it follows, or ignores, by designing what/how it operates; then in the individual demand that activates it, since human agency is the *prima causa* for its operations. Reflective judgment precedes machine learning by selecting and arranging what data is employed to train the AI; its replacement of human labor then creates the 'society of leisure' through the restriction of human agency to making reflective judgments (design). This intellectual labor has been the exclusive domain of the higher, "leisure" classes whose activity is ideologically separated from the drudgery of labor. When AI eliminates the necessity for human labor to perform the labor of determinative judgment, it elevates the lower classes to partial parity with the dominant classes. The ideological contradictions this change creates defines the barriers to any resolution of the social, cultural, political and economic crises created by the post-labor economy: the 'society of leisure' paradoxically undermines the heritage of the Enlightenment by proposing its democratic expansion to all of human society.

Acknowledging the range of applications for automation and autonomous agency is crucial to understanding this crisis, since altering the cultural differential between immaterial or intellectual labor and material facture will have a greater impact than the economic advantages of the technology. The emergence of the 'society of leisure' lies within this cultural framework and its central role for reflective judgment, but will also take far longer to appear since an ideological barrier determines the cultural impacts of AI. Any changes to the societal hierarchy are also necessarily a fundamental challenge to the asymmetrical power and social order of capitalism.

The critical barrier is a contradiction between the capitalist conversion of human agency into the commodity of "labor" and the Enlightenment elevation of agency as the vehicle for self-determination and ethical human action. This conception of ethical responsibility expands the significance of agency beyond its economic role as a mechanism for limiting distribution, and its role as the material creation of commodities, or in the emergence of surplus value from exchange. The freedom to choose how to direct one's agency encompasses both reflective and determinative judgment. The capacity to shift between these roles is an expression of consciousness, and the autonomy it postulates is an issue of ethical responsibility; in contrast to this freedom of human agency is the capitalist surrender of agency to the orders one is given—the definition of labor that exchanges agency for a wage. The Enlightenment ideal of ethical responsibility rendered as a political mechanism defines the basis of democracy in the actions of a rational, informed electorate, as well as enables the proposition of an egalitarian social order, and the assumption of rational decision making for economics.

Industrialization adapted this ethical dimension of agency to justify social and class differences as reflections of a moral failing specific to labor. Nineteenth century capitalism hijacks the Enlightenment concern with the self-determination provided by agency in the ideology of "autonomous achievement" that converts all actions into instances of individual responsibility. The denigration of labor is thus guaranteed by the societal hierarchy that emerged under industrial capitalism, reified by a religious sanction: the "Protestant Work Ethic"[127] involves confusing sympathy with empathy, an excessive faith in the power of personal agency, and makes a fetish from immediate experience that denies the more powerful impacts of structural bias in unearned and inherited privileges.[128] It perverts the cultural separation developed by Enlightenment philosophy between mind and body—distinguishing reflective judgment and determinative judgment—to conceive of labor externalizing their agency for a wage as a "refusal" to consider their ethical responsibility. However, separating the ethical demand imposed on all human activity from the legislative action of determinative judgment creates a contradiction: labor is virtuous when following the orders given—it is the definition of labor that they do as they are told. But the refusal to make ethical choices by surrendering one's own agency in 'following orders' is a self-conscious failure that philosopher Hanna Arendt termed the "banality of evil."[129] The requirement that labor exercise ethical decisions renders them immoral, while not making that evaluation also renders them immoral, placing labor in a double bind that reinforces the societal hierarchy.

This immorality of the lower classes was associated with their poverty and understands their difference from the higher classes as their own moral failing; it manifests as a denial of structural demands apparent in the belief that social, cultural, political, environmental, and even economic problems can only be fixed by personal changes to individual actions, behaviors, or habits. This ideology justifies differences in power, position, and class distinction by blaming the lower classes for their lesser position in society, transforming the technological unemployment created by AI into an individual difficulty, rather than a dire social outcome of a disruptive technology and making the elevation to the 'society of leisure' a cultural conflict over ethics and the appropriate role for the different social classes. Challenges to the societal hierarchy are threats to the rights and privileges of the highest levels of society, producing a blockade which will impede any easy resolution to the shocks and displacements of the post-labor economy.

§ 4.1 The Problem of Production–Distribution–Consumption

Equitable, democratic, and efficient mechanisms of commodity distribution do not exist. The first crisis of the post-labor economy emerging from AI and digital automation supplanting human labor will always devolve to the economic issues of distribution, an immediate concern with commodity access and utilization that hides the challenge confronting the established social order. Understanding the paradox that every AI creates for *production–distribution–consumption* illuminates the social and cultural problems of the emerging 'society of leisure.' Consider a "hypothetical" application of existing AI technology, the autonomous vehicle, used to replace human drivers operating tractor-trailers, the multi-axel, interstate shipping trucks that handle much of the long-distance commodity transport over land. In 2017, there were approximately 3.5 million truck drivers in the United States, with an estimated total of 8.9 million people directly employed in trucking-related jobs;[130] in a country with ~220 million people, this comprises ~4% of the population. Although these jobs may not be the most typically "exposed" to replacement,[131] the substitution of AI for human drivers offers significant advantages, both economic and societal. An machine can drive continuously twenty-four hours a day, seven days a week, and it does not develop fatigue or fall asleep at the wheel, making its use much safer and more efficient generally; however, truck drivers are an essential economic input in the many small communities they pass through while traversing their routes in the United States. The money they spend in transit provides an essential economic support; as long as the redundant human driver serves as a back-up copilot the impact of autonomous trucking will be limited, but once those drivers are eliminated and the autonomous vehicle drives its route by itself, additional impacts will begin to manifest themselves as a new migrant population arriving in the cities looking for work, a domestic diaspora whose impact will recall the horrific exploitation described by John Steinbeck in *The Grapes of Wrath*, a novel about the struggles of migrating tenant farmers and sharecroppers who left their Oklahoma farms in the 1930s during the Dust Bowl. These new migrants will be a collateral impact of AI even though their jobs have *not* been automated. To some extent, this exodus from small towns to the cities is already underway in the United States.[132] This migration into the cities is an economic, political, and social change whose cultural impact is entirely separate from the labor being automated, evident as a loss of tradition and "ways of life" that disappear. This hypothetical thought experiment suggests that whether automation actually replaces *all* human labor is irrelevant to its cultural impact, since the social, political, and economic crises will arrive as products of its collateral effects; replicate this technological unemployment with much higher paying, professional work that AI more typically impacts and the effects will be even more pronounced.

The force magnifier posed by AI accentuates already existing ideological contradictions, exacerbating existing structural inequalities between labor and management rather than resolving them through/ into the 'society of leisure,' even though that development is a potential result that may eventually emerge from this idling of human labor. However, in the short term, AI promises only crisis: central to the cultural, economic, and political order is the question of commodity distribution—access to the materials that serve both needs and desires is of central concern precisely because it is the most visible symptom of class difference. The historical mechanism that manages, constrains, and limits distribution is 'currency' shared through the cycle of wages::profits. These structural processes match the Enlightenment idealization of rationality enshrined in human agency as the source of all value through the assumption that this cycle is governed by rational actors making informed, intelligent choices; the role of agnotology in debasing and blocking rationality renders this assumption highly questionable in digital capitalism.[133] However, the historical understanding of the social relationships assumed by this valorization depends on the commodity nature of currency: that this token of exchange represents completed labor, a receipt for physical production that *has already occurred* (the conception of currency as being "backed" by a commodity). In digital capitalism this commodity-basis no longer applies to currency, whose unbacked, debt-basis reconceives currency as a title to *future production*.[134] This transformative redefinition of currency as the ability to demand production identifies how the problem AI poses for the social order emerges through commodity distribution, since the role of wealth that dictates that distribution is not only connected to material need but to social position and status. The transition to a post-labor economy emerges because AI disrupts the cycle of wages::profits. Unemployed labor cannot convert their wages into consumption if there are no wages—the exchange process depends on those wages being paid to labor to valorize the products of physical and immaterial facture;

this circulation ultimately depends on the human agency replaced by AI. The emergence of post-labor means that the vehicle for this cyclic exchange—currency—must be provided via an alternative to wage labor, i.e. by some palliative mechanism that replaces employment, such as "universal basic income," or the established system of production–distribution–consumption will collapse entirely while simultaneously concentrating wealth at the top of the societal hierarchy in a pathological fashion for social, cultural, and political order.

Oppression is always a product of human activity, and depends on human agency to happen; this capriciousness of individual action is what gives the 'objectivity' of AI its utopian appearance. This mechanism seems to avoid the cultural refusals of aid that are typically framed in moral or ethical terms in those societies historically dominated by Christianity. Religion justifies the societal hierarchy of capitalism via a prohibition on idleness explicitly stated in their holy book as 2 *Thessalonians* 3: "Those unwilling to work shall not eat." (Similar restrictions arise in other cultural traditions, such as Confucianism.[135]) The ideology of "autonomous achievement" and the "Protestant Work Ethic" reify this dogma originating in an agrarian society dependent on human labor that is entirely incompatible with the post-labor economy. It poses a barrier to the emergence of the 'society of leisure' by justifying the continuation of existing restrictions on access to production. This dogma is apparent in Schumpeter's observation of the belief "those who cannot climb by these ladders [of success] are not worth troubling about"[136]—the 'material needs' posed by poverty, homelessness, and the precariat composed from poorly paid, often informal, or on-demand labor without financial security[137] are signs of this ideology. The cultural problem of post-labor arises because solving 'material need' alone does not address the structural differences enshrined in religion, politics, and the societal hierarchy. Neither does fixing it produce a fairer, more egalitarian society, nor any variant of justice—but addressing 'material need' and creating a just society are not mutually exclusive; they are parallel dimensions of the same social oppression that restricts commodity distribution.

AI is a disinterested machine that seems to provide an autonomous 'Rousseauian archangel' that can correct these distortions of culture and the capriciousness of human desire that are at fault for creating all the ills of society. It is a replacement of the human agency that causes the imbalances, injustices, and disenfranchisements of the social order. The utopian fantasy is simple: an unintelligent machine can replace human fallibility to achieve a just society via an instrumental corrective to human avarice—it sees AI as fundamentally an instrumentalization of an ethical demand, the mechanical inheritor of Enlightenment concerns with agency divorced from human foibles. This utopian world where everything works as it should is an infantilizing fantasy where "the good and hard-working" would get exactly what they deserve, and everyone would behave properly, respecting their role as dictated by their class. This anti-capitalist fantasy of an "end of scarcity" and restoration of a idealized world is an infantile surrendering of responsibility to an authoritarian mechanism that is recognizable in the aura of the digital denying physicality and the material limits of technology; it is an argument for AI as parental mediator that dictates solutions to the problems of society. Surrender to autonomous machinery is not a "solution" to the imbalances of capitalism.

These fundamental cultural barriers to the post-labor economy lie with the expression of societal hierarchies that restrict commodity distribution, in their most extreme cases, by even denying the fundamental need for support to those individuals who cannot otherwise achieve subsistence. The cultural relationships abstracted into production–distribution–consumption are an emergent result of complex social, political, and economic interactions with private institutions, the apparatus of the state, and the societal hierarchy those organizations defend. These interests of capitalism and democracy are not convergent, as urban planner Richard Foglesong explains:

> The capitalism-democracy contradiction is an external one, originating between the political and economic structures of a democratic-capitalist society. More specifically, it is a contradiction between the need to socialize the control of urban space to create the conditions for the maintenance of capitalism on the one hand and the danger to capital of truly socializing, that is democratizing the control of urban land on the other.[138]

Foglesong is concerned with urban planning and land use, yet the contradiction he describes is a structural conflict over resources, their private ownership, and their social role that precisely describes the problems accruing to AI and the automation of production in the 'society of leisure' where the material production necessary for social reproduction excludes human action. What has historically only applied to the management of land and the shared, common features of the built environment (such as bridges, streets, the sewer system, electrical grid, or the digital technology of the Internet) becomes with the emergence of post-labor a general state of social organization as the mechanisms of production increasingly will depend on the same public supports for their operation and maintenance through an economic replacement for the cycle of wages::profits. To some degree these conflicts between corporate ownership and democratic oversight have already emerged in capitalism as the opposition between industry and government regulation. The invention of agnotology is a mechanism to forestall this social responsibility by rendering dissent and opposition ineffectual. The incompatibilities between the concerns of property owners and the democratic demands imposed by non-owners will manifest through conflicts over the planning process: this conflict is the "capitalism-democracy contradiction."[139] The political transition to the 'society of leisure' makes the mismatch between democratic processes and the structural demands for growth (accumulation and circulation of exchange value) evident as a collision between capitalism and the social demands for justice, equality, and legal protection.

The disproportionate power relationships of management versus labor raises questions about a fair allocation of resources in the post-labor economy. Discrepancies in the display of wealth reifies the societal hierarchy via the relative scarcity of production[140] that ironically becomes hyperbolic with the immortality of digital objects whose immaterial and instrumental nature renders them infinitely reproducible without decay or loss. The artificial incompatibility between new and old software reflects how the economic necessity for the "obsolescence" of digital objects is not assured except by design; thus, the control imposed by DRM becomes a mechanism of social control and dominance that instrumentalizes and reifies the societal hierarchy. The issue of cultural organization creates a model of rights and privileges based on fixed factors within the digital system itself, imitating the order of banking— access via investment; the lost access to analogue media is also required by this capitalist marketplace. DRM thus performs a cultural function as the mechanism of difference—expressing the societal hierarchy through the *which* and *what* of utilization and consumption: this historical hierarchy was simultaneously articulated through the differences of cost that restrict distribution, a rarefication of consumption dependent on wealth, and mirrored by the role of "waste" performed by the dominant classes as evidence of their success and position, aspects of the established order that conflict with the democratic proposal of post-labor and its elimination of human agency from the productive work of facture. The contradiction equally posed by weak or strong AI for wages::profits and distribution exposes the question of class and status in the emergent 'society of leisure.' Class conflict is guaranteed by changing sociological relationships, as those who have privileges attempt to deny their expansion to those who do not.

§ 4.2 Immaterial Control Over Moral Rights

The imposition of artificial scarcity on digital facture—via restrictions by digital rights management (DRM), existing intellectual property law, and the subscription model for access rights (utilization controlled by a tiered payment system familiar from banking)—demonstrates the inadequacy of existing social organization in confronting the democratic expansion of production that autonomous digital systems and AI present.[141] Their application not only to the products of digital technology, but to the technology itself constraints access, reaffirming the historical limitations on utilization imposed by physical access to commodities (valorization). The need to restrict access to immaterial production arises out of the problematics of valorizing intellectual labor that is readily reproduced and manipulated by digital technology, as lawyers Christopher May and Susan Sell explain in their study of intellectual property:

> Intellectual property constructs a scarce resource from knowledge or information that is not formally scarce. Unlike material things, knowledge and information are not necessarily rivalrous, and therefore coincident usage seldom detracts from social utility. Whereas two prospective users must compete to use a material resource (And this competition may be mediated through markets and the setting of a price), two or more users of any particular item of knowledge or information can use it simultaneously without competing.[142]

All the restrictions created by copyright, patent law, DRM, et. al. act to reinforce the established power imbalances that historical capitalism depends on for its maintenance of order. With the potential for infinite reproduction created by digital technology, scarcity ceases to be a function of facture, becoming instead a product of access and control over who is allowed use of the commodity/technology. It is a supplemental form of control that accentuates the restrictions already imposed by wealth over access. The change implied in this shift anticipates the problems posed by the post-labor economy and its need to restrict facture/performance that replicates the same problematics already in play with intellectual property. However, this technical imposition of scarcity differs from the historical scarcity of physical commodities or their restricted availability mediated via wealth which was based in the limited availability of production, yet these variants of DRM retain the historical imbalances apparent in the cultural order and affirmed by the societal hierarchy as what law professor Sonya Katyal described as the emergence of "semiotic disobedience." Artificial scarcity creates a new order:

> two coexisting and ultimately converging markets—one legal, and formally protected by the laws of property; the other illegal, and therefore vulnerable to criminal and civil sanction. And yet the difference between these marketplaces of speech—one protected, one prohibited—both captures

and transcends the foundational differences between
democracy and disobedience itself.[143]

This dualism reiterates the familiar positions of management and labor,
wealthy and poor, powerful and powerless. The opposition between
protected and prohibited marketplaces of expression Katyal describes
is now often policed by varieties of DRM, those digital systems that
automate varying degrees of agency in their operation. The content
management systems of social media, such as the video sharing site
YouTube, make this autonomous control into an explicit apparatus.
The role of AI in DRM is to evaluate the ambivalences and complexity
of allowed uses requires the flexibility of reflective judgment, but
these machines only render a determinative decision, exacerbating
the problems Katyal describes. These autonomous judgments
impose technological valorization/censorship divorced from the
necessary ambiguity of human decisions as a uniform assertion of
ownership rights; it is an implementation of AI as precisely the fantasy
'Rousseauian archangel' that can arbitrate rights and wrongs. The
copyright management tools for the video streaming site *YouTube* are
typical of these implementations. While there is a human-based appeals
process that allows challenges to these automated decisions, it is an
extra-legal apparatus whose actual enforcement of control depends
on the automation of claims employing model works uploaded to the
system; for example, to assert ownership of a video, a song, or other
media work within this system, it must first be made available within
that system by uploading the work to create a "Content ID."[144] It avoids
the existing system of copyrights entirely, substituting itself for existing
legal authority. Ownership rights only extend to those who are willing
to provide their media to *YouTube;* asserting a right *not* to be included
within the system is disallowed by its automation, even if the video
itself is not viewable by the "public"—its inclusion remains "hidden"
within the *YouTube* database.

The automated control over intellectual property creates a paradox:
rights holders wishing *not* to have their works on *YouTube* do not have
that right if they wish this system to respect their rights not to have their
works on this system. Supplanting legal rights with a privately owned
apparatus attenuates the rights the legal system addresses. Autonomous
agency is central to this system of control; yet it is also a system whose
operation requires a *de facto* surrender of the artist's moral rights that
DRM is supposed to be protecting. The same paradox defines the fiction
of 'artificial scarcity' when confronting the systems that enforce its
control. Opting out of the system is impossible; use of *YouTube* as either
audience or author requires acceptance of this mechanism, expanding
the market disjuncture Katyal described in 2006. The addition of AI
as an enforcer of the opposition of legal and illegal expressions via

controls over the social uses of intellectual labor shows how the digital automation effaces the artist's control over their work:

> Moral rights are thought to be both economic and non-economic in nature; that is, they are designed to protect both the reputation of the artist, as well as his personal interest in the work. The concept of moral rights traditionally includes three different facets—the right to disclosure (which allows a creator to decide when a work is ready for public dissemination by affording him or her sole rights in an incomplete work); the right of integrity (which protects against alterations that would interfere with the work's spirit and character); and the right of attribution (which protects a creator's right of recognition and authorship for a work).[145]

The autonomous control system employed by *YouTube* is a mechanism of valorization and censorship only concerned with economic rights. The moral integrity of the artist's right to disclosure is necessarily violated by AI systems that, like digital capitalism, infiltrate existing social order and replace it. The "Content ID" forces a surrender of rights to the database whose contents are a source of economic value for the company that controls it. The issue of moral rights makes the failing of DRM in "Content ID" self-evident as the "use/mention paradox" described by philosopher Arthur Danto in discussing "dangerous art" where all instances of use for a commodity—even that required to identify it—converge in the valorization process that is the database, creating new commodities (data) derived from the original work:

> There was a time when, under law, the quotation of obscenity was itself obscene, so that for a certain class of utterances, the distinction between what logicians term "use" and "mention" is dissolved. [...] You can't mention certain words without being perceived as using them.[146]

The most famous examples of the "use/mention paradox" are all illegal, such as obscenity, because their presentation collapses our ability to talk about a subject into the presentation of that subject itself—this dimension of censorship acts in precisely the same ways that employing DRM to police an artist's moral rights necessarily involves ceding those rights to a machine, and by extension to the capitalists who own/control that machine. Making the work publically viewable is optional, but withholding it from this valorization is impossible. That *YouTube* only polices economic concerns lies with how the database generated by this content management tools is itself a valuable commodity built from another's property. It is completely derivative: what gives this privately owned commodity (the database) value depends on the information it contains. Unlike a publically managed and owned database not created to generate profits, such as the registrations held by the copyright office, this technology valorizes the artist's work as protection for those rights to valorization. The *YouTube* "Content ID" facilitates valorization, with the predictable result that other types of moral rights are tangential to its operation; this technology gives no option to maintain moral rights, restrict access to that work, and avoid inclusion within this expansive acquisition of data. The "use/mention paradox" emerges from this automation of control, but the commercial exploitation of the work created by DRM technology is independent of the work itself; that it is a commercial property whose terms of service are subject to revision without notice places the potential abrogation of moral rights outside the realm of simple redress as a necessary feature of how these rights are privately administered.

Moral rights are secondary to the construction of this system. DRM systems such as the *YouTube* "Content ID" were created as a mechanism to accommodate and prevent piracy—rather than to provide other forms of control differentiated from exchange value. The practical problem posed by this required disclosure is that commercial theft of work is always a potential for anything held in a database— what has been put into the database can always be removed. The role of economic control is so dominant in systems of digital rights management that it is difficult to imagine a system *not* constructed in furtherance of these rights:

> When you upload a piece of intellectual property to *YouTube*, you need to create a representation of it in each of these [DRM] components separately. In other words, a single piece of intellectual property has up to three representations in the *YouTube* system:
>
> > 1. An *asset* is the representation of your intellectual property in the rights management system. You specify ownership and rights information as part of the asset.
> >
> > 2. A *reference* is the representation of your intellectual property for Content ID matching. You provide a digital media file that Content ID compares to uploaded video content.
> >
> > 3. A *video* is the representation of your intellectual property on *YouTube.com*. The video's metadata describes the content and specifies how it appears on *YouTube.com*. The video uses the same media file as a reference.

> The asset is the heart of the system, the object with which
> the other objects are associated. You must create an asset for
> every piece of intellectual property; references and videos
> are optional.[147]

The three types of control are interrelated; while the "reference" is not
a publically viewable copy of the work, it is nevertheless a complete
exemplary residing within a database of "information" (a library of
other completed works) that becomes the intellectual property of
YouTube, forcing an implicit transfer of rights to the corporation. The
function of machine learning in controlling access to works depends
on their "knowledge" of the work as an a priori identification without
which the system does not work at all; this is the necessity for rules (the
"reference") provided by inclusion in the database—the problem is the
private ownership of that database creates an economic value that is not
paid to the artist; unlike a public registry, the private system abrogates
the rights it seems to affirm. The need for the "reference" is a technical
dimension of these systems: its nature as a copy of the complete work
is obvious from its distinction from the "asset" which corresponds to
"metadata" for the material contained in the "reference":

> An asset contains information about intellectual property,
> such as a sound recording or a television episode, that a
> content owner has provided YouTube for rights management
> on our platform.[148]

Digital rights management systems are parallel, extra-legal entities
created and owned by the corporations that build them. The assertion
of ownership over the materials uploaded to YouTube to assert control
over intellectual property becomes a process of ceding the moral
rights to control the work and exempt it from YouTube. The artificial
scarcity affirmed in this system has nothing to do with aesthetics. It
is not an issue of imagination, but of property relations; questions of
intentional presentation and the experiential nature of a work fall far
beyond the scope of what AI polices with DRM. The issues of copyright
enforcement and management that accrue to YouTube (or example) are
symptoms of the usurpation of actions and roles that formerly were
exclusively the domain of governmental duties. It is a transfer of legal
authority to the private mechanism of a corporation. Acceptance of this
system where the undemocratic and unaccountable mechanism of AI
replaces public legal order increasingly forms the substance of social
experience in digital capitalism, making their operations into a fantasy
of ethical rights protection.

The social implications of defining AI as an eternally vigilant
censor who examines all utterances, images, and ideas to determine
if they are allowed explicitly creates an authoritarian culture whose

management is concentrated in corporations whose utilitarian calculus shifts intellectual property law from a foundational balancing of opposed values through reflective judgment (human cognition) to a determinative judgment based in the operation of an algorithmic match between database and immanent exemplar. Instead of creating a broader and more robust marketplace of expression, it automates the mismatches of cultural power that Katyal described in parallel and converging markets, one legal and the other illegal. This precariat of expression affirms the historical separation between producer and consumer that the interactivity of digital technology has weakened. This reassertion of traditional roles matches the instrumentalization of the societal hierarchy: the enforcement of property rights through DRM is an attempt to valorize each social use, every performance, all displays of intellectual property, resulting in a restrictive arena of speech where moral rights and commercial rights become interchangeable, and the cultural functions of media are strictly limited to opportunities for collecting rents/profits through pervasive monitoring.

§ 4.3 The Creative Act

The Enlightenment's elevation of ethical questions about human agency, shown by Kant's descriptions of determinative judgment and reflective judgment, began a cultural process that split agency into two separate roles, each linked to a different social class. The fundamental creative role of reflective judgment (management) was reinforced by the evident proof of empirical science and its direct application in the industrial revolution; while the application/audience for this work was left to determinative judgment (labor). The 'hatred' and provocation of the audience by avant-garde movements such as Dada exposes this denigration of labor as a feature of Modernist aesthetics: it acknowledges the intelligent role of human agency–as–director of productive activity is a central concern of art, then parodies this belief in/by the nihilism of Dadaist performances.[149] It echoes throughout the emergent Modern and its visible cultural formations, abstraction and formalism, both of which match and mirror the same class distinctions employed in the factory to separate the work of design from the labor of production. The conflation of these cultural and economic demands is apparent in architect Adolph Loos's manifesto/argument for the restraint of decoration in production, written in 1909:

> The evolution of culture is synonymous with the removal of ornament from objects of daily use. [...] The supporter of ornament believes that the urge for simplicity is equivalent to self-denial. [...] Ornament is wasted manpower and therefore wasted health. It has always been like this. But

today it also means wasted material, and both mean wasted capital. [...] The change in ornament implies a premature devaluation of labor. The worker's time, the utilized material is capital that has been wasted.[150]

This early proposal of formalism by Loos is operationally a manifesto. It promotes a restrictive type of production where the skill of labor becomes entirely secondary to the directive action provided in the design created by management. His claims occupy an important, prominent position in the development of formalist art and Modern design of the twentieth century; he describes tendencies that will be dominant by 1950. His rhetorical connections between ornament and crime, as well as his argument for labor's moral degeneracy that matches the divisions of reflective and determinative judgment, gives the signifiers of traditional skilled craft a negative connotation by linking them exclusively to the productive activities of labor and the lower classes. What his manifesto/argument identifies as "waste" is precisely those decadent, superfluous aspects of production that are inessential for the physical construction of the work in itself, but which served as signifiers of the skill and ability employed in production—thus they were identifiers for the contributions of labor to the design: "wasted time" in production corresponds exactly with the profligate ornamentation shown in/as the commodity itself.[151] In eliminating these aspects of production, Loos is proposing a type of facture that does not depend on the skill of the craftsman, but is instead an elision of their skill that mirrors the Taylorist restriction on the 'degrees of freedom' afforded to labor. What is produced in Loos's argument requires a minimum of time, materials, and labor—thus maximizing profits by reducing wages and material costs. It is an argument proceeding through moral and aesthetic foundations to defend an increase in surplus value. At the same time it enables a greater volume of commodities produced in the industrial factory. Enframing these claims as an ethical directive masks class differences as an aesthetic argument: he denigrates lower social classes and the necessity to translate his designs through the human intermediaries (labor) required for facture.

His argument for a formalist redefinition of aesthetics is able to increase production because less skill is required for the undecorated commodities he promotes, allowing the emblems of unskilled human labor to become the new signifiers of aesthetic value: for example, the prevalence of hammer marks in the arts and crafts movement's metalwork being produced at the same time Loos creates his argument act as a signifier of 'honest hard-working manual labor,' but at the same time do not require a high degree of skill to produce.[152] These arguments redefine the concepts of beauty, talent, and innovation as expressions of reflective judgment; the dominance his proposals achieve by the mid-twentieth century demonstrates their fluid contextual nature pushing alternatives aside. His formalist aesthetics are clearly a transfer of the organizational priorities of architecture (Loos was an architect) to manufacturing, and to art. The deskilling of traditional craft labor that began with industrialization accelerates under the premises of his Modernizing argument that strips away all decoration as inessential waste and immoral excess, allowing the maximal use of labor's productive time toward the fabrication of more commodities, rather than a smaller number that require both more time to produce and a higher degree of skill in production. By the mid-twentieth century, this rejection of 'skill' had converged on the issues of content in art, with a corollary rejection of the concept of craftsmanship for execution of 'serious art,' as artist Ben Shahn explains:

> Coming at length to the differences between the two works, the critic pointed out that the *Book of Kells* was motivated by strong faith—by belief that lay outside the illuminated page. But Pollock had no such outside faith, only faith in the material paint. Again, the *Book of Kells* revealed a craftsman-like approach, but no such craftsmanship entered into the work of Pollock.[153]

Ideology separates the determinative labor of production from the reflective labor of design—the precondition for "genius"—to dictate this characterization of Jackson Pollock's drip paintings, making his 'paint handling' a literal process with automatic results, rather than a painterly technique dependent on his craftsman-like virtuosity: this claim that there is no skill in Pollock's drip paintings renders them an autonomous accumulation of materials that makes any comparison to other works irrelevant and futile, a rhetorical assertion of the Romantic conception of artists as standing apart from physical concerns (such as the labor involved in craft).[154] This confluence of Romantic claims and Modernist formal aesthetics separates the meaning of the art from the object itself in precisely the same way that Loos separates decoration from design, evident in the ideological claims made about Pollock's work that specifically excludes both content and technical craft from the work on display.[155] These comments elaborate on Loos elimination of decoration as an aesthetic that makes the role of managerial judgment (design) central to the commodity by devaluing the creative contributions of labor. The ability of the art world—the network of critics, galleries and museums—to reinscribe the artists' work in their own terms without the artist interfering in that reinscription affirms these aesthetics and art itself as expressions of the *status quo*.[156] This reduction recalls the rote functions of the assembly line as well as anticipates the demarcation in *Conceptual Art* between the creative agency of the artist and the perfunctory role of skilled professionals in executing those designs.

Formalist rejections of decoration in art reflect the same cultural demands that inform industrial and architectural design. But unlike the economic decision that eliminates decoration, for art this same elimination descends from claims about a revelation of a "true" reality only visible to the mind, a transcendent product of Kant's reflective judgment addressing hidden truths, as formalist art critic Roger Fry recognized in the developments of early abstract painting on view in London in 1912:

> [These painters] do not seek to imitate form, but to create form; not to imitate life, but to find and equivalent to life. By that I mean that they wish to make images which by the clearness of their logical structure, and by their closely-knit unity of texture, shall appeal to our disinterested and contemplative imagination with something of the same vividness as the things of actual life appeal to our practical activities. In fact, they aim not at illusion but at reality. The logical extreme of such a method would undoubtedly be the attempt to give up all resemblance to natural form, and to create a purely abstract language of form—a visual music.[157]

Fry's metaphor to explain these alienating aesthetics, "visual music," is common to artists and writers addressing the development of abstraction. His review considers a range of *Fauvist, Cubist* and other avant-garde paintings by Henri Matisse, Pablo Picasso, André Derain, Auguste Herbin, Jean Marchand, and André L'Hote that makes their movement toward abstraction into a reflection of attempts to present the "reality of the mind."[158] This realism 'born of the mind' avoids the accusation of being merely decorative by asserting a transcendental significance—that they are revelations of an unseen, spiritual order hidden from normal vision by the everyday vividness of "actual life."[159] These aesthetic demands expressed through a transcendental Romanticism connect the economic choices that maximize profit to the distinctions and hierarchical separations of social concerns in a demonstration of the pervasive unity of capitalist relations in industrial society; it is a inescapable, expansive ideology that promotes an economic end, the increase in profit generation. This nexus of economic, cultural and aesthetic concerns immediately before *World War I* corresponds exactly to what graphic designer Paul Rand would theorize as "good design" in 1946, after *World War II*:

> Visual communications of any kind, whether persuasive or informative, from billboards to birth announcements, should be seen as the embodiment of form and function: the

integration of the beautiful and the useful. In an
advertisement, copy, art, and typography are seen as a
living entity; each element integrally related, in harmony
with the whole, and essential to the execution of the idea.[160]

Rand's proposal of "good design" as having the same aesthetic
qualities for billboards and birth announcements is a description of the
International or Swiss style in graphic design that emerged from the
exile of *Constructivism* from Germany and the USSR in the 1930s.[161] It
is an approach whose origins lie with the same reduction of ornament
and elimination of "waste" that Loos proposes. This devaluation of
the markers for craftsmanship—the "waste" of labor that creates an
ostentatious and inessential display of production—is an elevation of
the managerial design process employed in the rationalized factory.
The imposition of a fixed and invariant formal description of tasks to
be performed suppresses the creative agency of the labor that performs
the actual production; this dominance is the "scientific management"
proposed in Taylorism. This cultural imagination understands agency
in highly restricted ways that prioritize the novelty of creativity and
originality of thought—Kant's proposal of "genius"—that makes the
functional role of AI in executing designs the logical terminus of these
trends: a mechanism that performs precisely and only the instructions
given to it by management. The homology between the design and its
implementation by this technological apparatus brings the machine-
like roles imposed on human labor by scientific management into
consciousness as a dehumanization, an alienation not only of labor from
their agency, but from their intellectual capacity. The ethical failure posed
by the "banality of evil" thus requires a rejection of this subservient
position by labor, a fundamental refusal to submit to the structural
demands imposed by the ideology of "autonomous achievement."

'Creativity of production' is exclusively the domain of management.
The "degrees of freedom"[162] granted to labor are insignificant to the
capitalist system, a positioning that enables the minimization of labor's
agency in production through Taylorism and the structures of the
assembly line, while at the same time enabling a rhetoric, the aura of
the digital, that denies the role of software in the implementations of
AI. The separate roles for artists and labor recreates the separation of
management and labor in the factory; the use of automation and AI
does not alter this division of activity, but it does allow the fantasy
that the directives contained in the design are reproduced accurately
in facture, a 1:1 correspondence. Digital capitalism valorizes creative
agency (reflective judgment) that designs what the machines produce,
extending this agentistic role to the creation of software, but in doing so
entails a devaluation of the now-common role of software as a general
purpose tool. The extension of these developments to further address

the products of automated systems brings this consideration back to its origin point: 'creativity of production' applies equally to facture and to design—this proposition is in opposition to the received Enlightenment primacy for managerial control—for AI, it makes the operation of machine learning into an essential creative dimension of production, one that makes a consideration of the algorithmic aspects of this process as important as its outcomes.

The ethical issues this question revisits for automation in art proceed differently when addressing the automation of AI than when considering the role of labor's agency in implementing those instructions: it is not a question of the artist's creative design (reflective judgment), but of refractive and determinative judgments in implementing those instructions made possible by machine learning. This strictly determinate operation makes the critical study of AI into an ethical evaluation of its instrumentalities, because the behavior of the machine following rules is less important than which rules inform those operations, and consequently, whose values are rendered by that rule set. The prejudice of "implicit bias"[163] dominates autonomous agency because it reifies ideology–as–instrumentality into a set of fixed, unalterable constants in a way that biases, however implicit they may be, do not limit human cognition. The ambivalences of human thought that are difficult to quantify are nevertheless distinct from the regularity and predictable results of how AI automates determinative judgments—the very felicity that differentiates human agency from machinery is that aspect of interpretive consciousness that Taylorism seeks to eliminate.

§ 4.4 The Responsibility of Machines

The questions of responsibility and guilt are rarely asked about digital systems. Yet in their automation of determinative judgment it becomes the only ethical question that matters for their disposition of society. The issue of justice posed by AI ultimately depends on the mundane operations and daily, immanent experiences of the people who live in the 'society of leisure.' The twin fields of the personal and the structural define the social domain in distinct, converging, but not overlapping ideological frameworks that interface in individual experience, creating the particular conditions for each of the myriad subjects in society. Their distinction counters the ideology of "autonomous achievement" that explains any crisis or challenge— whether political, economic, social, ecological—as the exclusive product of *individual* responsibility. This isolation of structural objections in individual experiences does not challenge nor change those structures; it reinforces them through sound and fury, signifying nothing; thus deflecting any questions about the entrenched role of the societal hierarchy and its distribution of power. The capacity to differentiate between the personal and the structural is an essential precondition for any political action, critique, discourse. Distinguishing between these domains reveals digital automation in both weak and strong AI as a prosthetic agency created to meet a structural demand in capitalism originating with the need to expand profits, but always responding to individual decisions about implementation and control.

Cultural challenges to the post-labor economy encounter ideological barriers that accentuate rather than reduce the social, political, and economic crises of the emergent 'society of leisure,' preventing any simply solution. The ethical question of responsibility for the operations performed by any AI system confronts these barriers through its distinction from human agency. Yet the human deferral apparent in the helpless surrender to "the computer says no" captures this misplacement of responsibility onto the mechanism precisely: crime and lawlessness do not exist for a digital system that is confined to following an *a priori*, fixed rule set. The utility of these transfers / denials for the *status quo* is immediately apparent; AI is an apparatus that abdicates responsibility. The machine does what the humans who constructed it designed it to do: it is *only* they who can be guilty, who are responsible, not the unconscious mechanism no matter how independently it operates.

Responsibility makes the real distinction between human labor and autonomous systems self-evident: implementation by humans is a thought process that must adjust its activity to meet the demands imposed, it is not just a rote following of orders, as Arendt's argument about the "banality of evil" makes explicit. Both weak and strong AI implement what the humans who own the machine and benefit from its operations demand; they are the ones who must be held responsible for its operations. The fantasy of objective disinterested contemplation enshrined in autonomous function reveals itself: it is the aura of the digital, the belief that facture done by digital technology is a seamless process, rather than one fraught with difficulties, malfunctions, and limits imposed by programming and human desire.

These ethical dimensions posed by AI redirect attention back onto the databases used in machine learning, or into the results of the mechanism's operations, because the role of the computer in translating instructions happens at two removes from the human agency that constructs the device. First through the programming and creation of the software / hardware combination, then in the setting up of the instructions that system follows—an implementation that does not avoid labor's interpretive 'creativity of production,' merely displaces it to *a priori* construction of the machine and its operations. This distancing of effectuality from human action is not an elimination of the skilled professional. It disguises the skill of human agency (design) as the machine itself, a dispersal that protects management from the results of their actions that transform AI into mechanisms of autonomous oppression.

The unconscious machine is never responsible, cannot ever be responsible. The human tendency to surrender to the impartiality of the computer—to abdicate responsibility to the faceless, nameless, entity of the machine and its creators—acknowledges the heritage of industrial capitalism and is a recognition that this autonomous system is also an authoritarian one. Although it is constrained to perform whatever it is built to do, the labor using the device rarely has any control over its operations, being instead a benign interface. It is an automation of the historical Taylorism that leaves the labor operating these systems with few options to make moral or ethical decisions, leading to a systemic learned helplessness in face of ethical or moral responsibilities. But the builder is responsible in equal measures to the one who sets the device in motion, rather than the labor whose activities constitute its functioning. This doctrine of responsibility is the mirror image of understanding human agency as the *prima causa* of all production. Even for the AI system created through machine learning, this initial decision about the database is deterministic, the final arbiter of responsibility, and the necessary locus for any judgment about the device's operation must lie with the ones whose decisions determine the system, rather than the impersonal system itself.

§ 5. AUTONOMOUS INSTRUMENTALITY

The potential of autonomous agency to create a more just society depends on how its impacts are accentuated or diminished by its implementation. Suggesting an emergent 'society of leisure' from the idling and dismissal of labor entails an expansion of reflective judgment, but at the same time both weak and strong AI have applications that instrumentalize the social divisions between classes that diminish this leisure. This application of autonomous agency to sorting and directing agnotology::surveillance entangles a perverse, self-reinforcing cycle of intrusive corporate and state power. The valorization of human behaviors through preprogrammed social interactions increasingly hide these forms of authority by disenfranchising the human agency subjected to them. These reifications of control through determinative judgment operate as a performative mechanism that changes capitalist ideology and the societal hierarchy into an algorithm of dominance that implements the difference between the manufacturer of a machine and its user as an assertion of asymmetrical power. Digital technology restricts human actions to a proffered set of *a priori* options, perversely creating an appearance of human efficacy while controlling those behaviors in advance by defining their scope: all AI systems operate as a "magician's gambit." Human agency is captured in the apparent freedom of choice given by the system, when every available option actually provides no real choices at all. The simplest variety of "magician's gambit" is a stage illusion where the performer asks someone from the audience to choose between two things—it doesn't matter which is chosen because the outcome is predetermined. Select the prepared option, and the performer will go to work on the selection "doomed with a word," but select the other and they will "spare that one" and go to work on the first option that was not selected. It is an appearance of freedom of choice, without there being any freedom or choice at all. The options provided were simply a ruse. AI implements this same process in a more elaborate schema that simultansously restrains and valorizes human agency. This process allows no more freedom of choice than the "magician's gambit" does, bringing all human demands under the same control as the assembly line to establish a new form of alienation specific to digital capitalism.

Surveillance is essential to the autonomy of all machine learning and the interactive capacities of every AI: the human agency at the foundation of this process must be transformed into data to allow the interpretations generated by the machine to proliferate in direct response to the expansion of data collection, driving the valorization of the database and its productive operations that save as much of this data as possible for as long as possible, an assumption of value which follows the cultural expectations of the infopoor society that more information will result in better decisions. Accumulating data derives from historical societies where data is scarce, but it is contradicted in the contemporary inforich society created by digital technology and constant, on-demand access. The vast stores of data present material costs in storage and their value is always based on their potential application in the future. Where these 'databases' of information (the archive) in infopoor societies helped to establish certainty and resolve debate, in digital capitalism they promote agnotology through the paradox of choice and information overload. Instead of creating greater certainty and moving towards consensus, the superabundance of data results in 'decision paralysis'[164] and an abandonment of reason for a purely emotional, irrational selection guided by affect. In place of a rational, democratic process of informed judgment and stable decisions, agnotology emphasizes the irrationality and fleeting caprices of feeling. It is the same decision making process described by psychoanalyist Eugen Bleuler in his discussion of the pathological ambivalence of schizophrenia.[165] His dual definitions of this ambivalence for schizophrenia in the emergence of a cognitive superposition makes the 'irrationality of agnotology' apparent as an exploit of normal thinking:

1. *Ambitendency,* which sets free with every tendency a counter–tendency.

2. *Ambivalency,* which gives to the same idea two contrary feeling tones and invests the same thought simultaneously with a positive and a negative character.[166]

These definitions for mental dysfunction identify it as a feature of human intelligence, a side-effect of how the mind handles ambiguity and ambivalent situations. Schizophrenia exaggerates typical situations into the superposition of opposed potentials that agnotology exploits by blocking interpretative flexibility through an acknowledgment of the incompleteness of our experience and knowledge, undermining the adaptations which enable us to act without complete knowledge. We do not typically experience these limits because our experience of the world *is* the limits themselves.[167] This structural insecurity allows agnotology to force human judgments to rely on emotion rather than reason to make rational choices: the issue is not truth or falsity, but undecidability (ambivalency) created by confronting radically different but equally credible accounts for what is superficially the same thing. Agnotology expands for the inforich society because the *un*certainties discovered by surveillance only serve to demonstrate an ever greater number of alternative potentials. This network of recording, observation, and human action is mitigated by the autonomous instrumentality that will always discover its own limitations, whatever else it finds—failings that can only be addressed by more and expanded monitoring that intrudes ever deeper into formerly private domains.

The personal is political.[168] Digital capitalism colonizes social domains using algorithmic systems to transform what were merely rote determinative judgments into a fixed set of conditions and results, an instrumentalization of social behavior that allows for a robust denial of responsibility for the actions of these systems, giving their cultural impacts the appearance of an essential, natural order beyond human capacity to effect or change. Pervasive monitoring traps human agency as material for valorization—it does not matter how many choices, or which choice (if any) is made, so long as it is recorded in the database. Humans can only select from within a limited, given set of *a priori* options; this passive observation alienates human agency by defining its choices in advance and then rendering those choices moot. The result is the same no matter which option is selected—the essential feature of the "magician's gambit." Imposed, commercial applications of AI by companies such as *Facebook* or *Google* finds its corollaries in the individual selection of the same processes in, for example, the automatically restrictive matching of online dating[169] used by companies such as *CoffeeMeetsBagel*,[170] *Match.com*,[171] or *eHarmony*[172] that limit their customer's potential matches by facilitating individual preferences for race, religion, sexual orientation, physiology, economics, as well as less immediately relevant or obvious factors such as genetics.[173] Homogenous self-selection created by class and cultural difference becomes instrumentalized through these uses of AI as an essential mechanism for turning data collection and management into an operative system of social order, a refractive sorting of human society. This cultural impact emerges directly from human choices—personal decisions—made about *how* AI will sort, match, and organize data, with the result that these systems reinforce social conformities and accentuate cultural differences by using them as criteria for exclusion. This technique for reducing disharmonies isolates groups from each other, preventing conflicts not through mutual understanding but by an autonomous and invisible digital apartheid.

Pervasive monitoring imagines the creation of certainty though continuous observation and analysis following formal logic, while its counterpoint, agnotology, undermines these same intellectual procedures used in the creation of knowledge. Automation and AI are instrumental in valorizing both surveillance and agnotology, rendering them invisible through the immediacy of their operation: the value of a single search online, or even the act of walking through a store, increases the value of the database created by surveillance, an apparatus of control that, like the telescreens of George Orwell's novel *1984*, offers "no way of shutting it off completely."[174] This intrusiveness is essential to the operation of the AI device in itself: without constant autonomous surveillance, the weak AI of digital assistants such as *Siri* (from *Apple*) or *Alexa* (from *Amazon*) cannot respond when called upon. Their surveillance is specifically instrumental, but their "always on" nature expands surveillance into ubiquity, normalizing it. The moment of dominance comes through the cultural internalizing of surveillance as an essential feature of each individual's own "private" social life as performative, valorized commodities, apparent in the spectacle of images on social media such as *Snapchat* or *Instagram*. In Orwell's novel, the telescreen was provided by the state even if you didn't want it; in contemporary digital capitalism people *want* to pay for their surveillance device (smartphone) and seek out the newest, most powerful models that promise to become even more intrusive. In concentrating corporate power digital technology employs the surveillance of social, economic, and political action as a mundane part of everyday life—it maintains the established order, preventing the emergence of alternatives, while its complement, agnotology, creates affective palliatives that dissipate what cannot otherwise be contained.

Thus, the "privacy" offered by digital technology is necessarily a farce and fantasy.[175] Pervasive monitoring is central to the operation, valorization, and authoritarian control performed by AI; the economic value of data collated in the database provides an immediate structural motivation for both the claim to respect privacy, and offers a powerful incentive for its violation. While no single piece of data is itself a source of value, the aggregate produces surplus value without wages through the use of the database. An illusion of privacy acts as a marketing tool for expensive technology that the user/owner does not fully control. The highly publicized "privacy" controls offered by the *iPhone 11* are a demonstration of this tendency—the controls to "turn off" the location monitoring in this cellphone do not completely deactivate this monitoring. This mismatch between the user control and the operation of the device is a design choice by *Apple*, as security researcher Brian Krebs explains about this device:

> This week *Apple* responded that the company does not see any concerns here and that the *iPhone* was performing as designed. "We do not see any actual security implications," an *Apple* engineer wrote in a response to *KrebsOnSecurity*. "It is expected behavior that the Location Services icon appears

in the status bar when Location Services is enabled. The
icon appears for system services that do not have a switch
in Settings."[176]

Why this activity happens is irrelevant. The human owner of the device
does not fully control its operations—the "system services that do
not have a switch" are hidden functions performed by the machine
that the user cannot control. It raises the immediate question, *"What
other functions are there that have not been disclosed?"* The containment
of human agency arises from how this device creates an expectation
that the user's actions control the operation of the machine; however,
the appearance of control is not the same as actual control. "System
services" continue to track and identify location even after that
function has been "deactivated"; the user control over this function is
imaginary—the controls in the *iPhone* "system control panel" do not
match the operation of the device itself. This discrepancy reveals how
the software required to operate these devices disenfranchises their
human operators who perversely must pay for the privilege of their
own tracking and extractive valorization in order to reap the benefits
of contemporary digital society. What or how this information is or
is not being used is irrelevant to the illusion of privacy it produces;
the discovery that this function is by design makes the other privacy
invasions performed by *Apple* devices, such as their built-in facial
recognition technology and the pervasive monitoring by the digital
assistant *Siri* further examples showing the "magician's gambit" is a
fundamental protocol for the implementation of autonomous systems.
What matters in the operation of autonomous digital machines is the
demands made by their designers. This separation of control from
ownership is an expansion of the division already apparent in the 'right
to read' created by DRM: *Apple's* products establish that it is possible to
'own' the device but have no real control over its operations. By making
pervasive monitoring ubiquitous and mundane, paired with the lack
of actual control over the operation of everyday devices, the fantasy of
privacy and efficacy which the *iPhone* demonstrates shows the digital
normalizes disenfranchisement and the alienation of human agency as
simply the "cost" of using these technologies.

Surveillance is a uniform mechanism that allows weak AI to
perform complex tasks such as affect recognition, speech recognition,
facial identification, or reading license plates on the street. The specific,
individual nature of the task being automated is inconsequential—it is
the process of data collection for semiotic manipulation and machine
learning that defines these operations. Performing these agentistic tasks
gives AI an ever-expanding, gradually more central role in the security
apparatus that also creates a demand for additional types of intrusive
social valorization.[177] This colonization of social domains arises from the

limitations of determinative judgment when confronting *unknowns*—situations posed by and requiring reflective judgment (human reason and agency). The degrees of freedom, just like the illusions of control and privacy, that result from this instrumentalized social order are only superficially liberating: the 'society of leisure' does not preclude either the use of AI for commercial or authoritarian purposes. The operations of digital systems simply reflect the demands made in their construction and application—dimensions of technology determined in advance by human choices (design).

Both weak and strong AI are neutral technologies. There is no necessity for any particular application of these devices in production; machine learning makes its distance from the human judgments it reifies into the superficial autonomy of its actions obvious. The disinterested operation of an unintelligent machine only appears to be 'objective' because it mediates, however directly, the human agency that constructs it and sets it in motion. When employed commercially, this apparatus can create unique experiences for customers through predictive algorithms that anticipate their desires and needs, thus accentuating and encouraging the generation of surplus value. It can also perform a political role as an autonomous police force monitoring public spaces for "precrime" via continuous surveillance of those individuals whose class, race, past actions, or current behavior renders them suspects even when they have done nothing illegal.

The substitution of AI for human labor in what were cultural or social assessments of individuals, as with the evaluation of employment applications, the detection of criminal behavior, or deciding financial evaluations such as loan approval, gives the role of AI in social relationships an insidious character. AI's entanglement with pervasive monitoring and agnotology creates a mutually reinforcing system of control, mitigating social disruption. This result or application is equally a product of the same process of monitoring, identification, and automated response that defines how the new, digital alienation captures/valorizes human agency, diminishing the significance any action performed by converting it into uniform data, thus alienating the human agency it captures. Ironically this dispersal of human agency by AI enables a democratic expansion of "leisure" that allows labor to assume the same cultural position as management.

Maintaining the societal hierarchy through the autonomous control of AI paradoxically counteracts the potential for transformative change posed by this elevation without eliminating its cultural, economic, or political disruption of the *status quo*. The disenfranchisement and capture of human agency by these machines not only mitigates the capacity to challenge the established order, it renders the challenges ineffectual. How these devices invisibly affirm the *status quo* demonstrates the need for rational human evaluation of their operative systems to mitigate historical prejudices masked in the database, as well as avoid automating persecution via the operations of these machines.

§ 5.1 Instrumentalizing Implicit Bias

The unconscious operation of AI has the same appearance of 'objectivity' that all digital production has—but biased data always and only produces biased results, "garbage in: garbage out."[178] Any belief that "data isn't political" is a fallacy; how data is collected, described, exhibited, fabricated, sorted, and preserved derives from internalized assumptions whose normalized biases about what is significant defines "expertise."[179] These problems with data collection and its use in general, and for the construction of AI via machine learning, are obvious and consequently well-known.[180] However, the potential dangers arising from the autonomous implementation of implicit bias[181] is what makes the secrecy in their construction and operation a critical issue: the algorithm is not just a proprietary technology whose value depends on it remaining hidden from examination (thus from challenge); its deployment also relies on the opacity of the database itself created by superabundance of data itself to maintain the illusion of objectivity. The overly exhaustive presentation of data is an opportunity to mask bias and hide prejudice through the appearance of comprehensive, transparent documentation—this aspiration to instrumentalize the state of information defines the aura of the digital and its erasure of physicality. The same fallacy that 'data isn't political' describes the displacement of bias effects in machine learning by increasing the dataset. This attempt to efface the ethical dilemmas of autonomous agency via an illusion that they can be resolved through more data ignores how ethical issues are reflexively dependent on the particulars of use rather than an essential concern with the conditions deployed in themselves.

The limitations of the database necessarily assert the assumptions enframed by the pervasive monitoring that creates the database itself, which then propagates into the autonomous system via machine learning as the parameters of its operation. Bias becomes the mechanism of operation, an invisible transfer that only emerges from a careful examination of the machine's outputs—the results of its automated action. Ethical problems posed by AI are always immanent to its applications. The case of bias in the ranking algorithm used by the United Health Group, Inc. (UHG) is a useful example of this transfer between biased data and the instrumentalized prejudices being magnified by machine learning. These structural biases were rigorously studied by Ziad Obermeyer, MD, et. al. in their examination of instrumentalized bias and its technical implementation.[182] This medical software used weak AI to prioritize patients for receiving additional care, but its implementation transformed a structural, racial bias hidden by differentials in wealth into an instrumental system where white patients automatically received preferential treatment. The identification of this bias makes the UHG ranking algorithm a useful example to consider the role of bias in machine learning. This case reveals how the assumptions about the standardization of data converges on the abstracting principles guiding the historical Taylorist fragmentation of the industrial assembly line. The mechanisms employed in digital automation differ in the nature of their activity, but not in their procedural organization and elimination of significance from those operations on the database. This transition matches the presumptions of scientific management: that the problem of bias merely lies with human judgment, rather than the structural demands that constrain those decisions. Automating determinative judgment by/as the algorithm enables the reification of the existing caprices, but masks this transfer behind the aura of the digital.

The internalization of bias is the definitional moment in achieving expertise.[183] Implicit bias becomes an instrumentality reified as AI, but it is not a problem of these machines or an unintended consequence, it is their primary function: the UHG system prioritizes patients to receive additional care—the problem is who was being prioritized and who was not. The UHG ranking algorithm identified a racist, structural bias contained in data it was trained on, a result of that data using health care costs as a proxy for health care needs. UHG automated existing racism inherent in spending more for the health care of white patients than for black patients, resulting in white patients being preferentially ranked for additional care ahead of more gravely ill black patients. The problem it created was a problem that already existed. By ratifying the societal hierarchy expressed through economic differences in spending, AI turned that bias into the instrumental action of an autonomous system (via the algorithm), thus placing its structural racism beyond easy critique or recognition.[184] These failings of data and training are familiar and well known examples of instrumentalized bias.[185] The issue UHG poses is the question of a fair and equitable distribution of the medical care it schedules for patients, apparent in the ways the ranking algorithm prioritized patients who were less sick because of flaws in the training data. The solution proposed to this problem is more pervasive monitoring: to correct the flawed data involves replacing it with different values or with more data, as Obermeyer, et. al. note in their concluding remarks:

> Rather, we must change the data we feed the algorithm—specifically, the labels we give it. Producing new labels requires deep understanding of the domain, the ability to identify and extract relevant data elements, and the

capacity to iterate and experiment. But there is precedent for all of these functions in the literature and, more concretely, in the private companies that invest heavily in developing new and improved labels to predict factors such as consumer behavior.[186]

However, this positivism assumes that the perfection of digital systems can overcome and eliminate bias—all that is required is more data, better data, data separated from social demands, or otherwise distanced from the demands of human desire. This "fix" invents a justification for expanding pervasive monitoring more deeply into the social realm, reducing ever more human activity into data–for–valorization. The consequences and danger of unanticipated and unintended bias on judgments developed through machine learning is inherent to the operation of these systems; the biases in the UHG system are likely present in other systems as well, making the need for oversight and public, peer-review of these instrumentalities essential. The bias identified in the UHG system elicits a greater awareness of the hidden dimensions of social injustice, but correcting the algorithm invites an expansion of this "fix" as corrective for social failings, a process of censorship and restriction that engages in "image-blaming": the proposal that removing the offending representation, a symptom of a harm, is the same as redressing the harm or acting to prevent it happening again.[187]

Arguments for justice and equal access do not vanish because an autonomous process makes the decisions, nor do the structural biases of the societal hierarchy disappear because a machine no longer enacts them. The surrender of reflective judgment to a determining process supplants the role of human society in performing these same tasks. Without critical access to the algorithms making these decisions, their implementation is simply a hardening of whatever bias is contained in their training data. It reveals the paradox at the heart of this problem: that AI systems however independent of society they may appear to be are constructed from the same social relationships they are being used to serve. The attempt to eliminate the biases in a social construct by abstracting that same system, but refusing to engage the mechanisms erected to provide a just resolution to its conflicts leads to the instrumentalization of bias—ageism, bigotry, chauvinism, exceptionalism, nationalism, racism, sexism, et. al. Prejudice is an internal dimension of human society that requires a continual discourse to identify and address. In being instrumentalized, this discourse of reflective judgments collapses into a fixed social organization.

§ 5.2 Social Accountability and Restricted Access

The creation of an "Algorithms Management and Policy Officer" in the City of New York is clearly an early attempt to address the issue of instrumentalized, implicit bias at an institutional level through pubic accountability.[188] However, the task of this new office that oversees AI is complex: structural bias becomes a feature of the AI's operations only if it is a failure of how the system was created, rather than a transient glitch or mistake—as with the UHG system, the prejudice must be a common outcome of normal AI functioning to be as instrumentality. The homologous link between the training data, its sources in pervasive monitoring, and the operations of the system means the AI will necessarily also resemble the social order, a factor that makes identifying structural bias both an explicit necessity for oversight of the algorithmic system, and simultaneously a discovery of social inequities expressed in/by the data itself. The capacity to challenge the results of machinic action is attenuated by the removal of human judgment from the operation of these autonomous systems; reaching a human who can make a correction is essential to the redress of automated harm, but complicated by the intransient nature of the algorithm itself, often forcing these corrections to be personal corrections, individual in nature rather than addressing the structural expression of the machine itself.

Further *de jure* legal protections are a familiar part of how industrial capitalism protects itself from both competition and oversight.[189] The control granted to corporations by copyright, patent law, and the ambivalent legal status of pervasive monitoring achieved through end-user agreements makes oversight of the foundational dimension—data and the algorithms trained on it—effectively impossible without a new legal framework specifically being created to allow oversight and control by government rather than industry. What problematizes these legal attempts to redress the operative bias of these machines is how the action of machine learning is always a matter of instrumentalizing prejudice and automating the divisive process—because that *a priori* categorization is the nature of the refractive judgments they replicate, and simultaneously defines the instrumental role of expertise. Nevertheless, the greatest barrier to peer-review correcting structural bias in the implementation of AI is commercialization. The value of these applications depends on a two-fold restriction on access: first, in the data and database that makes machine learning possible; then, through the algorithms that define the AI itself. Divergences from an egalitarian ideal are hidden by the opacity of these systems to external oversight, and the difficulties posed for legal redress by the human subjects they administer.

The conversion of the societal hierarchy into the immanent orderliness of monitoring is implicit in the automated prejudice of the UHG ranking algorithm. The emergence of biased contingencies in the operation of these systems may be an unavoidable consequence of their derivative nature—they rely on data created from past social and cultural behavior. The questions to ask of the biases apparent in the UHG case are manifold: whether this prejudice is unwarranted or unjust, and so requires redress beyond just "fixing" the machine; the extent of the harm it has caused; is it only a function of the training data, or is this bias a structural problem crystallized from existing ideology. The UHG system reifies the *status quo* societal hierarchy in its scheduling additional medical care internalizes existing structural bias via machine learning, and then rendered as the instrumentality of AI. Demonstrating bias in these systems is difficult for precisely this ideological transfer, even though instrumentalizing bias is a well-known problem.

Structural bias may be an easily foreseen and corrected mistake, or an unanticipated and surprising flaw in the construction of these tools, yet at the same time this automated bias reveals the ideological function of these machines as mechanisms of social sorting and control. The UHG case demonstrates how machine learning provides a uniform mechanism for authority via refractive judgments that are simultaneously evidence for implicit bias in the training data. It demonstrates a societal hierarchy that serves white patients differently than black patients. As both weak and strong AI replace human labor, the instrumentalized biases defined through machine learning become difficult to correct not because they are hard to identify, but because they are dimensions of the 'black box' of automation protected from scrutiny by law and the obscurity of the technology itself. This incapacity to challenge the algorithm reveals how agnotology serves to counter any accusation of bias before it can be leveled because of this cultural assumption of objective impartiality. When the results differ from a democratic or egalitarian ideal, the corrective action that Obermeyer, et. al. suggest makes the potential uses of AI as a technology for cultural and social engineering obvious.

The obfuscation of bias is essential to the role of these technologies as mechanisms of social control; it also valorizes the mechanism even if the validity of the data it generates is in question. The use of AI for "affect recognition" makes this uncertainty essential since emotional responses are highly contextual: a smile can be friendly, happy, angry, ironic, sarcastic depending on the moment of presentation, making its evaluation complex even for human viewers.[190] The necessity to mask the operations of these systems enables their commercial exploitation with only limited restriction. This same necessity for obscurity applies to any database employed in semiotic production; however, the data sets specifically employed in training AI systems to perform complex agentistic tasks create new issues for the social dynamics they supplant precisely because the automated mechanism replaces the nuanced consideration possible with human labor. When these unintelligent systems follow the parameters generated from the data employed in their creation, they reify the implicit biases within that data, producing an automated version of the "observer demand" confirmation fallacy. *Who* creates the system becomes as important to its operation as the data since the demands of the programmers necessarily inform how the data is selected and framed for use in machine learning; the homologies of the computer technology industry deserve more careful attention— the issue of workplace "diversity"—the employee demographics of companies such as *Apple, Google, Microsoft*, or *Facebook* have been overall dominated by white men belonging to the same social class whose interests and concerns (as with any group in a position of dominance) become the implicit assumptions for how technology operates and whose interests it serves.[191]

§ 5.2.2 A Social Intervention

The ratification of the Enlightenment bias against determinative judgments is automated in the reified biases of AI that continue the *status quo* social order of capitalist societies. This action contradicts the egalitarian values of democracy. The opposition of capital and society is internalized in technology: this reified ideology is a factor that works against the correction of implicit biases contained in data, and counters the empirical tendencies of AI development seeking to minimize these biases. What drives the structural shift to this technology is an ideological distance between the decisions of managerial judgment and their execution by labor—those divisions of activity and authority that separate the "leisure class" from the drudgery of production.[192] The fantasy evoked by using AI to identify and correct social bias offers the proposition that creating more egalitarian instrumentalities will also correct the excesses perpetrated by human society, thereby creating a more just society through a transition to autonomously administered rights and privileges. This replacement is the aura of the digital offering a fantasy that AI can correct social and cultural ills.

AI realizes an ideological demand to transform societal hierarchies into an instrumentality that can then shield the established order of capitalism from challenge. The automation of rights through DRM, much as the surrender of rights this implementation demands, transforms social relationships into a system of obligations and privileges that form a fixed constellation of potentials and roles. The transfers of structural bias into the operations of AI is not a neutral development, even if it matches a systemic demand to maintain the *status quo*. The implementation becomes resilient to challenges—asking how many individuals were harmed by the UHG system's operation is the moral or ethical question of its impacts, but it is also secondary. The critical aspect to acknowledge about machine learning itself is that this system intensifies the established and dominant hierarchies expressed in existing property relations, historical racial and gender roles, and the separation of managerial and productive labor. The capacity to correct these imbalances makes the cultural threat of AI apparent.

§ 5.3 The Fallacy of 'Objectivity'

Invariance grants autonomous systems the mantle of objectivity, an essential dimension of the ideological understanding of AI as a pure instrumentality of the managerial will. This distanciation of the mechanism from the human agency that operates it matches the assumption made about photography in the nineteenth century. Because the machine performs its operations independent of the vagaries, persuasions, and excuses that can redirect human decisions once they have been made, the assumption prevails that these digital automatons match Sol LeWitt's comment that "Once the idea of the piece is established in the artist's mind and the final form is decided, the process is carried out blindly."[193] The apparatus follows the paradigm it has been designed to reproduce, never deviating; the results of AI assume the superficially impartial appearance of any inhuman mechanism that itself is unconscious, and in being unintelligent, mutely challenges to any human attempt to question its impartiality. *Conceptual Art* internalizes this objective criterion of machine operation as an aesthetic value, showing this convergence of 'objective' and instrumental behaviors. The danger posed by the biases of AI is precisely that holding them accountable for their operation confronts a double bind: in results of the machine's functioning, and then again in the operation-design of that system. Because an AI is trained by data that may itself be collected and aggregated by another AI without any obvious organizational bias, the unintended consequences of the machine's functions—such as a racial bias for prioritizing white patients over black patients—can be difficult to challenge or correct without having full access to both the algorithms, the labor they perform, and the foundational data used in its training.

'Objectivity' for autonomous agency suggests using the digital computer as a technical means to redesign society as a whole, employing it is a mechanism for 'social engineering,' making a robust discussion and debate over AI technology even more essential. Autonomy from direct human oversight appears to be an ethical, equitable and just replacement that will necessarily produce an objective and ethical outcome in society; this belief is a fantasy. The *un*responsibility of the machine is transformed by the aura of the digital into a virtue rather than a deflection or masking that allows for a human disavowal responsibility. The uniform operation of the system does not guarantee it creates unbiased results, yet this premise constructs a false equivalency between consistent function and lack of bias. Understanding human judgment as inherently biased precisely reflects the conception of digital automation: consider the example of the search algorithm employed in the *Google* search engine that employs a database whose contents are functionally secret even though the data is accessible to anyone who uses their technology. This compilation of data relies on being functionally open to any user, yet its internal operations *being-hidden* act as a mechanism to counteract any claims its results are biased.[194] Obscurity hides bias in the autonomous data collection and semiotic production of the database.

However, the data collected by *Google* is wide-ranging and expansive: surveillance records both the actions related to indexing material posted online, and describes the actions taken by users, including the information gathered by *Android*, which tracks and saves location data about user movements,[195] as well as a myriad of other factors that are not publically disclosed—creating significant opportunities for AI to invisibly instrumentalize bias without any possibility for oversight or examination. The claims made by *Google* about their search algorithm assert its independence from human oversight, suggesting that 'human oversight' is the source of bias, rather than the data itself:

> When you search on *Google*, ranking systems sort through billions of web pages in our Search index to give you useful information in a fraction of a second.
>
> These ranking systems are made up of a series of algorithms that analyze what it is you are looking for and what information to return to you. And as we've evolved Search to make it more useful, we've refined our algorithms to assess your searches and the results in finer detail to make our services work better for you.
>
> To give you the most useful information, Search algorithms look at many factors, including the words of your query, relevance and usability of pages, expertise of sources, and your location and settings. The weight applied to each factor varies depending on the nature of your query—for example, the freshness of the content plays a bigger role in answering queries about current news topics than it does about dictionary definitions.[196]

The autonomy from human control that *Google* asserts about the operations of its search engine is the same historical denigration of labor in scientific management, but expanded to apply to any social control over the operations of AI. The aura of the digital masquerades in this defense, obfuscating the instrumentalized bias contained by machine learning. This denigration of reflective judgment is an elevation of the determinative action of a rote machine, offered as a preemptory negation of any interrogation of how either weak or strong AI instrumentalizes the database: the identification of "ranking systems" by *Google* makes the complexity of its search algorithm apparent, but without providing any real insight into the "mechanics" of how it operates. This blockage of external analysis maintains the fallacy that algorithmic systems lack bias, enshrined as the illusion of their "objectivity," which justifies these systems' autonomous operation without external human oversight. Being driven by the data collected by pervasive monitoring, as in the *Google* search engine's operation, is a preeminent exemplar of this process of automated editorial control: the machine pretends to be independent of commercial or social concerns—a clear fallacy for a company supported by advertising and the manipulation of demographic data—demonstrating the fallacy of 'objective operation' as a justification for granting its results a *de facto* exemption from legal oversight.

AI makes ideological claims of independence and 'objectivity' for the fully rationalized judgments it pronounces. The aura of the digital expands this rigidly empirical appearance of impartiality to the database as well, since only those things quantifiable and encodable as data matter to this system. Operating as an unintelligent, practical power, both weak and strong AI determine neither morality nor happiness; human demands lay out the path this device follows as an *a priori* feature of how desire intersects with the data employed in its operations. If surveillance is parasitic on the human action it observes; the database is its toxic refinement that must be protected under a veil of independent objectivity, or the operations and power it enables will be rejected as illegitimate and untrustworthy. The valorization of surveillance and the data streams it produces are essential to commercial, criminal, political, and police operations. Without data, AI does not function. The automatic retention and maintenance of databases becomes a necessary part of the control network that places the AI system at its center: the necessity for more information, as well as the retention and application of any data already collected presents a structural barrier to any attempt to reign in the concentrated corporate power that employs agnotology::surveillance and AI as mechanisms of social, cultural, political and economic dominance. Agnotology enters into these dynamics as a defensive shield that obfuscates the database, its contents, and its operations by rendering oversight problematic and legal restrictions on deployment of collected data moot.[197] What is not acknowledged nor open to public inspection is difficult to challenge or critique—the ability to suggest that objectors to these combinations of AI and pervasive monitoring are paranoid or unreliable is a product of their obscurity that demonstrates agnotology undermining opposition.

§ 5.4 Social Control

The capacity to automate systems of social control emerge simultaneously in [a] the mobilization and direction of the carceral powers of the state, apparent in the interface between mechanisms of automatic policing such as the red light camera that issues traffic citations, and [b] the immaterial policing of behaviors provided by the invisible manipulations of what information and data are encountered through digital media. For authoritarian regimes, both these functions are consolidated in the state; for capitalist democracies they are shared between corporations and the state. Where [a] is concerned with a physical control over the body, [b] manipulates the mind. Both applications converge in the already implemented types of weak AI commonly in use as mechanisms entangled with agnotology::surveillance. The "magician's gambit" is one mechanism of control; the algorithmic selection of materials to present to an audience (autonomous editing) is another.

AI implements surveillance on a scale that is impossible for human labor unaided my machines; its commercial applications are only different in degree from its parallel uses in policing and security. The automation of judgments imposes orderliness on the chaotic morass of everyday experience that historically could not be monitored. Autonomous agency allows for an uninterrupted identification and tracking of individuals that was impossible in the past, thus instrumentalizing the conservative motivation to maintain social order: a creation of a 'predictive policing' system mandated with catching criminal behavior makes the application of this technology into a direct mechanism of social control. The development of biometric recognition technologies—technology that measures unique biological characteristics—has enormous potential to become a mechanism for continuous social manipulation and control through its capacity for agnotological disruption or the commercial domination of all aspects of life. This fallacy can expand the cultural gulf between the degenerate poor and the virtuous wealthy, enabling a constant monitoring of words and actions accompanied by automated demerits or other punitive measures. This political application reflects the neutral role of technology as a force magnifier: the data collection and processing made possible by AI allows the use of video surveillance as more than a passive recording of events, transforming it into an autonomous warden who identifies, catalogs, and punishes human behaviors in both public and private spaces. This use shifts the nature of social control from an internalized set of rules to being an imposed framework that is only followed because of the (inevitable) detection and punishment. Even simple technologies—such as the "traffic light" camera that issues citations for driving through a traffic stop, or the "speed trap" that can be automated to issue speeding tickets—are exemplars of AI deployed for social control and the autonomous application of political authority. The AI system only requires being set up and activated to begin detecting and then automatically punishing infractions. For example, a stolen car involved in a police chase that exceeds the speed limit and drives through traffic lights will generate citations for the owner of the vehicle even though they are the victim and did not commit a crime; the technical development and automation of oversight in public spaces renders authority as an impersonal, machinic operation exercising political power and state authority, but is not responsive to contingencies and the ambivalences of human life.

The commercial applications of this same system of political control is the proposal of a 'market of one,' a bespoke management of lived experience only previously experienced by the highest royalty—kings, queens, and their entitled offspring. These various commercial applications of the same fundamental technology entails a fusion of autonomous agency with pervasive monitoring to create a seamlessly solipsistic experience in the physical world where each individual's desires are anticipated and met without their necessarily having to articulate the demand nor needing to accommodate alternatives. It is the extension of the human-centric dimensions of automation whose operations depend on the agency of the human subjects-under-surveillance. The capacity of this technology to exacerbate the function of agnotology to isolate each individual in a 'thought bubble' that only contains things that they already know and believe, or alternatively, to manipulate those same individuals though the curation of what information they receive and which ideas they encounter cannot be denied. This management of contingent demand is precisely how these technologies are employed by "public relations": the design process that is "market-researched, audience-tested, vetted, modified, revetted and remodified" [198] described by Martin Scorsese. These same operational tendencies that reconstruct social and public behaviors as economic activities and demographic data already exist and operate via social media such as *Facebook* or in the promotion of 'related videos' on *YouTube* where algorithmic curation an selects materials that are more likely to retain their audience's attention and maintain their 'engagement' with the commercial product—generating revenue from advertising and from the human audience's response–selections.

The unintelligent nature of these algorithmic servants providing 'what their customers want' has protected the companies constructing and profiting from these technologies from liability for the contents they deliver to their customers based on the idea that they aren't editing or producing that material. In the United States, this protection is formally provided by Title V of the *Telecommunications Act of 1996* (section 230 in the "Communications Decency Act"), 47 U.S.C. § 230, which states:

> No provider or user of an interactive computer service shall be treated as the publisher or speaker of any information provided by another information content provider.[199]

The autonomous editorial operations of AI that control and manage the presentation of this information creates a distinct ambiguity around its 'objective' and 'disinterested' selections based on user demands, especially since the material provided by these "third party" speakers is not simply presented as a series of posts, but is instead commodified and packaged by the "provider." The autonomy of AI is not a closed loop. There is a distinction between materials contained in a series of otherwise uncurated materials and the careful presentation and selection of user–generated materials. The owners of these machines do control their operations through their control over the algorithms, apparent in their promoted delivery and sorting of materials seen by human audiences: what appears on *Facebook, YouTube,* and other social media platforms is not an autonomous product independent of oversight, but one that is managed and redirected by both paid positioning and the internal choices reified by the algorithm itself. This curation is an automated editing where the AI system magnifies the effectiveness of the controlling human decisions to enhance valorization through 'engagement': the automated editor selects what and when to show things and to whom, not based on a user-originated request or a "blank" selection such as chronology (putting the most recent things first, regardless of who they are from), but based on a hidden metric that only the company controls.

Considering AI in its role as an autonomous editor and mechanism of social control the editorial process inherently makes what is hidden and suppressed by the algorithm as important as what it does show. The choices about who is allowed to use the system and what they are allowed to publish through it is a contentious issue for all social media precisely because these companies do not consistently implement their 'acceptable use' policies uniformly. Censorship by companies such as *Apple, Google, Twitter, Facebook* or any other "distribution platform" should be recognized for what it is: a tacit and explicit admission of editorial control over algorithmic decisions and activities and their desire to use that technological power over information distribution and access as a form of social, political, and economic control that serves the *status quo*.[200] It is through the mitigation of access that AI becomes a powerful force in social relations, one whose dominance matches its political power as a mechanism of authority. These twin roles descend from the same procedural reification that solidifies the autonomous system as an extension of the human mind that designs it.

The role of AI in the presentation and organization of content displayed through digital technology gives the question of social control a saliency for considering the power of autonomous systems in managing dissent and creating contingent demand—not merely for commodities, but as a mechanism of political dominance and discursive redirection. The mitigation of information grants control over society. This dimension of automated social control descends through the capacity for AI to amplify misinformation generally, and create agnotology in particular. It is through the production of multivalent forms—works where several potential meanings simultaneously emerge in a work, sometimes at differing "levels" of interpretation—that allows ambiguity to undermine interpretation in a process that ironically eliminates potentials and thwarts human decisions by posing multiple and incompatible options. The operation of agnotology depends on this indistinguishability of fact and non-fact—a "relativism" that conflates antitheticals to eliminate the possibility of debate through an inability to separate fact from falsehood—a reflection of equivalence originating with the database and its instrumentalization of the state of information, beyond all considerations of validity, empirical reality, or dialectical opposition that renders all ideas and political positions identical. This collapse of established fact allows the continuation of the *status quo*, and that is the primary impact of AI curation: the ways it dis/ables agency, and who benefits from this breakdown are readily apparent in the social control and blocking of dissent produced by these mechanisms that more precisely and completely manage the flow of information than any technology before.

AI displacing human labor has specific cultural impacts as the post-labor economy expands the 'society of leisure' beyond its restriction to only the highest social classes:

[a] Human labor ceases to be the foundation of value.

[b] The means of production becomes a commodity in itself.

[c] The role of cultural authority held by 'gate keepers' increases.

[d] Currency becomes a title to initiate production, rather than a receipt for past production.

[e] The gamification of 'social credit' reifies the societal hierarchy as an instrumentality of control.

[f] The cycle of wages::profits requires social maintenance, as with other elements of the material infrastructure.

[g] The model for value production with reflective judgment (design) is fundamentally performative, and so is resistant to automation and increased efficiencies due to both the nature of art/design itself and the socio-cultural role it plays.

[h] Agnotology::surveillance intensifies as the valorization of social activity afforded by AI becomes increasingly employed as both mechanisms of social engineering and commercial exploitation (via contingent demand and the valorization of human activity).

[i] Traditional cultural ideologies are structural impedimenta to the transition and emergence of a 'society of leisure' through their demonization of inactivity, and justification of the historical societal hierarchy that emerged in an agrarian, infopoor society dominated by sustenance production.

§ 6. CONCLUSIONS:
THE SOCIAL AND THE AUTONOMOUS

All digital technology, especially the autonomous agency of both weak and strong AI, acts as a force magnifier where what might have seemed to be arguments *ad absurdum* about the contradictions between automation and human society, such as the potential for a post-labor economy where AI eliminates the need for all human labor in facture, instead now appear to be reasonable extensions and extrapolations of cultural, economic, and political impacts that fall within the realm of technical possibility. Inherent oppositions emerging in historical capitalism between the costs of living labor and the rate of profit that implemented the Taylorist preoccupation with minimizing labor's agency in production continue with digital capitalism and its use of automation. These ideological tendencies gives the transition to a post-labor economy credibility: the goal of "scientific management" is precisely this limitation and elision of human labor as an intelligent part of the facture process. The invention of autonomous agency makes what was a formal difference between the reality of a reduced role and this implicit goal of completely eliminating living labor simply a matter of degree. For processes such as the semiotic manipulation of a database, validating credentials, as well as labor-intensive rote processes such as speech and facial recognition, this replacement of human labor with weak AI has already occurred.

The aspiration in digital capitalism to employ the state of information as an instrumentality through semiotic production has rendered human agency moot. The colonial expansion of digital capitalism employs all AI systems as an extractive and exploitative valorization. These deployments create additional sources of value through pervasive monitoring that creates additional benefits for the technology companies constructing these machines. The capacity of digital production to rapidly, efficiently, and inexpensively generate commodities without the consumption of human labor, resources, and capital changes the calculus of what is argument *ad absurdum* and what is not. The post-labor economy emerging with digital technology is no longer simply a sci-fi fantasy or hypothetical extrapolation from current trends; its impacts are already apparent as the 'great decoupling.'

§ 6.1 Emancipating Human Labor

Post-labor emancipates human agency from the drudgery of facture and work in the mundane production of those things that sustain life by imposing on human cognition a consistent and uniform demand for the reflective judgments of management. The mechanism of this emancipation, automation, ironically frees human labor by recreating the social order of historical societies divided between masters who direct and demand production (humans) and slaves who must meet those demands (machines), but without the injustice and horrors of human chattel; however, this 'society of leisure' potentially created by the end to human labor is not a proposition of immanent utopia, a technological freedom from worry and distress. The proximate and inherited assumptions of historical and digital capitalism equally obstruct the discursive analysis of this development, substituting either twentieth century myth-fantasies of a worker's paradise, or fiscal objections based in contemporary assumptions about the nature and costs of labor and production. In considering these transformations it is especially important to ignore questions about "cost" because they are always proximate, connected to the immanent moment, rather than questions addressing the structural transformation underway: consider the "cost" of printing a full color photo-illustrated coffee table book. In 2019, the per unit cost to make only a single copy of a 100 page publication, produced on-demand, are ~US$12.00, a price point more determined by the cost of the paper and physical material than labor; in 1919, these costs are exponentially higher, so high that the production of a single copy is economically impossible (and cannot be done on-demand in any case); in 1819, the printing technologies used to produce these books make full color reproduction virtually impossible, and the technology assumed to be the "content" of this example—photography—does not exist yet (it will not even be invented until 1826). Which "cost" is the appropriate one to consider in addressing the use of printing technology for on-demand production? The radical changes described in this 200-year span express the fallacy in considering the issue of "cost" when addressing the impacts of technological change: "cost" is a contingency determined by the historical moment the question is asked. New, disruptive technologies that replace earlier time, labor, and materials-intensive processes with greater efficiency and reliability undermine the objections of "cost."

The structural shifts posed by the post-labor economy and its expansion of the 'society of leisure' cannot be addressed through a fiscal calculus. Cultural changes and societal reorganization into the 'society of leisure' developing from the automated displacement of human labor from facture are not a matter of *never*, merely of *not yet*. Ignoring this fiscal concern in considering cultural impacts shifts the discourse from the immediate questions of displaced labor, changes in taxation, and the problems of transition to the structural barriers derived from the societal hierarchy that with direct and determine the process itself. Understanding these cultural restrictions conceives the opportunity to choose how this change will proceed, a process that makes a more just society a possibility rather than only an idealized fantasy.

The distinction between a change in the role of human labor and an elimination of human labor in general is significant. 'Post-labor' does not mean humans are no longer working, but that human agency is no longer the foundation of value. The impacts of post-labor economy will appear long before all human labor has been eliminated from production. The redefinition of value this change represents means fundamental changes in the social order. Those populations dismissed become an absolute surplus, making the issue of "over population" into more than just a question of carrying capacity, but of social position, resource allocation, and commodity distribution. These issues are linked historically by the restrictions on leisure imposed by social class (and evident as differences in wealth). The legacy of the Feudal social order derived from the distinctions of lord/serf that have been maintained by the separation of management/labor is incompatible with the Enlightenment ideologies of self-consciousness and agency of democracy. The incompatibility between this order and the democratic expansion of the 'society of leisure' is obvious.

Machine learning creates automatons, exemplars of Karel Čapek's "robot"—a term which means "serf labor" in Czech—whose common use is derived from the title of his play, *Rossumovi Univerzální Roboti* (*Rossum's Universal Robots*, 1921), that designates an autonomous, forced laborer. The ethical questions posed by the structural contradictions between [1] wages::profits, [2] immaterial semiotic production and the demand for use, [3] the need for human agency quite apart from utility, [4] how agnotology::surveillance entangles the societal hierarchy with production, and [5] the difference between material utility and social utility are directly implicated in the organization/distribution of commodities within a society where human labor is no longer central to the generation of value. All these factors depend on Enlightenment philosophies of human agency and ethical behavior that were ratified in the development of industrial capitalism. These historical beliefs dovetail with traditional religious prohibitions on idleness and leisure in an ideological framework that opposes a general emancipation of human society from laboring. The *status quo* divides consumption and access to commodities according to a hierarchy that depends on the enforced labor of the majority for the benefit of a minority.

While the "Luddite Fallacy" clearly applies to some kinds of mechanization—the implementation of machine tools and automated processes which amplify and create efficiencies, but do not eliminate human labor—the creation of autonomous agency raises fundamental questions about the assumption that new technological innovations that eliminate human labor necessarily simply shift it to other sectors within the economy. This assumed validity for the 'Luddite Fallacy' remains true if and only if the invention of autonomous tools do not function in a fashion similar to human slavery—the "robot" is an unconscious agent capable of performing the same essential role as living labor, but without demanding compassion, empathy, or rights. The requirement to perform intellectual labor—historically the exclusive domain of human labor—is the difference between an automated and autonomous actor: the automated process requires the oversight provided by human agency, while an autonomous process, by definition, does not ("autonomy" means there is no required oversight).

The transformation of the social order that was slavery into industrial capitalism, whether the slavery of serfdom and Feudal caste societies, that human labor called "robota" in Czech, or the racial slavery of the United States, involved a change in valuation that enabled the consolidation of power and wealth in the mercantile class that comes to dominate with the industrial reorganization of both markets and production; the cultural change to industrialization describes a new dominant class assuming power over the same mass of labor oppressed by the Feudal lords.[201] Continuities between earlier social order and industrial society gradually emerged over the nineteenth century as the transition matured: the appearance of trade unions is the continuation of the historical craft guilds that organized skilled labor and policed production stand as an oppositional social force to the power of management; the denigration of labor is matched only by the demonization of labor unions in its consistency. The instrumentalization of productive agency in both weak and strong AI remains connected to these pseudo-Feudal distinctions between labor and management: an hierarchical organization whose authoritarian internal structure recreates the ownership of the Feudal lord (management) over the productive land (machinery) and the serfs who perform labor (both automation and AI). The emancipation of forced labor (serfdom) during the Enlightenment and the emergence of industrialization during the nineteenth century are reflections of the newly dominant emphasis on agency as the essential constituent for being–human; yet the conversion of agency into a commodity and its role in the creation of value serves to alienate individual agency from labor, concentrating it into the reflective judgments of managerial decisions. The devaluation of determinative judgment from its description in Kant's *Critique of Pure Reason* to the proposition of cybernetics by Ashby in the twentieth century describes the role of rules–based analysis and application as a rote action lacking in creativity and using intelligence in only a limited way; the facility of automating these decisions with the unintelligent processing of digital computers affirms their conception as restrictive forms of procedural activity. The devaluing of their agency corresponds to the alienation of industrial production.

Capitalist wealth creation has historically been founded not upon the imaginative activity of inventing new understanding, but in the dreary activity of applying established principles to produce consistent results, validated in/by the mass-produced commodity. Empirical science is a mechanical process. Even important discoveries and innovations, such as the incandescent light blub,[202] are not a product of sudden insight and understanding characteristic of reflective judgment, but the tedious and thorough action of data collection. Once a reflective decision has been made, its application is always determinative—the rote activity of scientific validation, where the result may be unknown, but the testing-observation procedure that creates data is constant. Although reflective judgment is much less necessary, its valuation is considerably higher than the activity performed in following and executing its application apparent in the differential in wages paid to the CEO and the janitor. This differential explains *whose* employment is at risk of being automated, as the *Brookings Metropolitan Policy Program* noted about the impacts of AI in November, 2019:

> The exposure curve [for jobs being replaced] peaks at the 90th percentile, suggesting that while middle– and upper–middle–class workers are likely to be impacted by artificial intelligence, the most elite workers—such as CEOs—appear to be somewhat protected.[203]

This revelation should not surprise anyone: it is unlikely that the individuals who decide how this technology will be used will voluntarily choose to replace themselves. The enormous wages paid to C-level or upper management are a signifier of this labor's rhetorical importance and value in directing production, a demonstration of their societal position that allows the consumption of leisure.

The distinction between reflective and determinative labor is reflected in their valorization, but wealth creation still depends on the productive activity of labor following *established* processes. However, their cultural significances are a mirror image of these productive relations: under the ideology of "autonomous achievement" only reflective judgment is highly valued, while the more rote and routine the activity of determinative judgment is, the less it is valued; those everyday activities necessary for sustaining life, being the most routine, thus come to be the least valued—mundane, rote activities such as vacuuming dirt off the floor were some of the first applications of machine learning to be available for the general public's own use.

The connections between significance and the societal hierarchy is reflected in the social changes occurring during the development of industrial production, noted in passing by semiotician Umberto Eco in discussing the changed aesthetic and cultural appreciation of serial works by the Modern audience emergent with industrialization:

> Modern aesthetics and modern theories of art (and by "modern" I mean those born with Mannerism, developed through Romanticism, and proactively restated by the early-twentieth-century avant-gardes) have frequently identified artistic value with novelty and high information. The pleasurable repetition of an already known pattern was considered typical of Crafts—not Art—and industry.[204]

What Eco identifies as the rejection of serial production is the cultural difference created by the Enlightenment's elevation of reflective judgment that distinguished the creative, original "genius" (novelty and high information) from the drudgery of determinative repetition typical of industrial production. Human agency becomes a philosophical concern central to the separation of management and labor, and its reification in industrial production further affirms this changed significance that articulates social distinctions between Kant's types of judgment. What makes the Modern distinct from earlier periods is its differential evaluation of productions that follow established rules (it involves little creative agency in forming new work) from productions that invent new rules. The 'law of automation,' where any activity that can be automated will be, follows this demarcation between the significant activity of reflective judgment and its implementation by labor: it affirms the societal hierarchy in which productive labor's contributions to significance have been consistently subservient to the demands of facture. To the cultural imaginary these relations are asymmetrical: the capacity to implement instructions are a different concern than the creation of those instructions.

AI is the ideal factory worker imagined in Taylorist scientific management, suggesting a fantasy of immediate realization, a direct correspondence between the agency that designs and the facture that produces—an elimination of the need to translate instructions through the intermediaries of human labor. This instrumentalism is the apotheosis of the capitalist valorization of agency. It is the "magic money tree" that eliminates the transformations and lost profits created by labor, leaving only the instructions of the creator in a direct relationship to the creation. The metaphysical significance of the ideology of "autonomous achievement" is self-evident in its demiurgic overtones and the imagined self-efficacy and self-sufficiency it projects. Narcissism and solipsism are appropriate descriptions for this belief in a Rousseauian independence from the demands of society rendered as an instrumentality. These features of the cultural embrace of automation should not be discounted or ignored; they are the most salient aspects of how the social translates the magical illusion of digital production into the familiar dualisms of action and reaction, appropriate and inappropriate, justice and injustice.

§ 6.2 Futurity and History

The twentieth century cultural preoccupation with futurity so highly visible in both the fantasies of popular science fiction, and the more elite avant-garde continues to shape the present even as concerns with 'the future' have grown darker and more apocalyptic in nature, a reflection of the cultural shift to the Contemporary described by C.B. Johnson that negates such futurist concerns of Modernism and Post-Modernism alike:

> In all of these attempts to think of the contemporary, we are
> faced with the unavoidably paradoxical: trying to recognize
> a condition that succeeds the twin megalithic codes of the
> Modern and the Post-Modern, while unavoidably
> cannibalizing those terms in the very act of reading into
> each dispensation of the contemporary. [...] what we are
> seeing in the enigma is the repetition of a category that has
> all the outward signs of Modernity—a commitment to
> now—but none of Modernity's future orientation.[205]

This *nowness* is apparent in the valorization of the future as a token of exchange, but it is also the liquidation and repression of the 'program' that defined the imaginary utopias-yet-to-be equally manifested in both Modernist and Post-Modernist conceptions of a new society. This disappearance is an implicit acknowledgement of a cultural change apparent in the futurity of currency: for any title to future production to be meaningful the present must continue indefinitely because the value of currency is pure futurity, created from nothing,[206] out of "fairy dust."[207]

This system of futurity–as–exchange suggests an emergent 'society of leisure' and which would serve the distribution needs of a post-work economy is precisely a barrier to its emergence. A concern with futurity and its implication of change masks how the shift to autonomous agency is not an end to capitalist hierarchies, but a hardening of them to opposition and challenge. This ratification of futurity is matched by an ahistorical liquidation of the past apparent in the random-access arrangements of automated search results based on automated assessments of "relevance" rather than importance or historical chronology. What seems a paradox or contradiction in these developments is not: the very value of this reconception of currency is predicated on there *not* being a radical upheaval that could render these tokens of exchange invalid. The assertion of a continual present implicitly demonizes the future (change), and is accompanied by the erasure of the past (history): for the present to continue there can be no accommodation of a teleological progression into presentness since that would suggest changes yet–to–come. It is a juvenile or infantile denial of "growing up" and the responsibilities that accompany it, as well as a rejection of death waiting at the end.

The post-labor economy challenges the historical foundation of value in human agency, a dramatic and essential alteration in the social order whose displacement of existing hierarchies is countered by the translation of those structures into an instrumentality that maintains the *status quo*. An evacuation of precedent and tradition featured in the artistic avant-garde of the twentieth century, anticipating this contemporary expansion where the "facts of history [become separate] from historical memory"[208]—an authoritarian feature of every avant-garde manifesto that rejects the past along with all of the art of the present that fails to comply with the movement's agenda.[209] This liquidation of the past allows its agnotological reconfiguration to suit any claim or demand made for it; the lack of historical memory is matched by the reconfigurations of the database, mutable and flexible, a reconfigured foundation for a tenuous and unstable present. The social engineering performed by the algorithmic capture of 'engagement' by AI depends on this ahistorical re-ordering for its optimal effect. The radical potentials of the post-labor economy thus come to serve the implementation of their own containment via legal policies and commercial applications that strengthen traditional institutions and norms by converting them into the orderliness that gives the instrumentality of the digital system its appearance of 'objectivity,' but conceals the received, internalized, implicit bias that is the *status quo*.

§ 6.3 The 'Society of Leisure'

Expansions of the 'society of leisure' that seemed like lunatic premises before AI no longer do so, but this change can only come from a fundamental transformation of ideology, ably articulated by the Enlightenment, and a reconsideration of religious dogmas that block the end to work, and are apparent in definitions of personal identity through labor and employment. These self-reinforcing cultural beliefs more appropriate for agrarian, subsistence societies converged as industrialization whose mass production reduced the scarcity of commodities and invented the labor–saving technologies enable the transition to a post-labor economy. The invention of autonomous agency renders this established structural order resilient to opposition and egalitarian replacement by transforming the societal hierarchy into formal instrumentalities of dominion, even as this reification undermines the social capacity to adapt to the changes the enforced idleness of labor produces. The desire for order and security, just like the need for fairness and equality, are equally transformed by the application of AI technology to "fixing" social ills into a fixed set of acceptable and unacceptable behaviors since determinative judgments are legislative operations leaving no space for ambivalence or change. The computer is a machinery for sorting and selecting from within data, not an egalitarian or impartial judge of ethics or fairness. Hardening social conventions does not produce resiliency, but instead creates a brittle order requiring constant demonstrations and reassertions to maintain its ever more tenuous power, an authority that seems more eternal, more fixed with each new demonstration of power, but instead becomes more subject to the instabilities it seeks to eliminate.

Wealth, the historical mechanism that has managed commodity distribution and enabled demonstrations of social difference by restricting access to commodities is directly connected to the managerial control over production. The dimensions of cost, access, and fairness articulated through how wealth limits distribution made inequality obvious in historical capitalism. With the emergence of a post-labor economy the mismatch of wages::profits forces a social change because wealth can no longer provide immanent symptoms for recognizing any individual's position within the hierarchy. Understanding an "economy" as the apparatus that distributes and addresses the material needs of its human population, the capitalist economy is foundationally dysfunctional, and the misgovernance it produces will only be exacerbated by being instrumentalized in AI. Accumulations of currency that signify wealth for the existing societal hierarchy become a pathological impediment to the stability of the post-labor economy precisely because they are entitlements to demand production, rather than stores of value: in a society where the performance of labor is inessential to survival, the "wasted" consumption of its products can no longer signify the same status position. This expanded 'society of leisure' creates new cultural conflicts over standing within the societal hierarchy that emerges from the alternatives to the cycle of wages::profits offered via governmental payments (whose sources always ultimately lie with some form of taxation), in capital that is never repaid (grants or via periodic jubilee that abolishes debt), or as obligations for future repayment (debt). All these options for managing distribution are extractive variations on the "rent" associated with wealth generation: they move and distribute existing values without adding new ones. Depending on the social organization of individual countries, these differences create a variety of results, some more egalitarian than others.

The cultural impact of these changes necessarily reflects the particular history of individual societies, yet the articulation of the 'society of leisure' is unmistakably underway as an international phenomenon, apparent in the shift from currency as the preservation of past value, to the role of currency as reified futurity—a title to demand production—that renders existing production a 'dead value' awaiting consumption. It expands the problems familiar from urban planning for both commercial and non-commercial social benefits to encompass the relationships between autonomous production technology and the social supports that enable it, as urban planner Richard Foglesong explained about land use in the 1980s:

> The market system [for infrastructure use] cannot meet the
> consumption needs of the working class in a manner capable
> of maintaining capitalism; [...] the inability of the market
> system to provide for the maintenance and reproduction of
> the immobilized, fixed capital investments (for example,
> bridges, streets, sewage networks) used by capital as a
> means of production [requires a non-commercial solution].[210]

The built environment is simply the most durable "standing reserve" in society. Unconsumed past production depends on contingent demand to mobilize it through exchange, a factor that only differentiates it from the fixed capital investment of infrastructure by the duration that passes between production and the need for replacement (consumption). Digital capitalism's reification of futurity as currency, the right to demand facture, aligns with the priorities of post-labor and its erasure of human agency from labor, but in doing so brings the differentials between capitalist demands and the social into prominence as conflicts over the disposition of production, the restriction of consumption, and the costs of its maintenance or replacement. These separations become increasingly apparent as the same distribution question that already confronts urban land use: how to coordinate the various constituencies that are impacted by changes to the use of what are not merely commodities or means of production, but shared infrastructures that maintain the society as a whole? The problem becomes explicitly political rather than economic, requiring a consensus between all the affected parties in democratic societies, a factor that makes the authoritarian tendencies of digital capitalism apparent in how the "smart city" has been proposed as a combination of AI, pervasive monitoring, and the privatization of democratic process to create dictatorial zones of corporate control—fully autonomous "cities" administered by corporate needs rather than democracy. This transfer reflects how democracy does not administer public goods in a way that is conducive to maximizing profit generation since its concerns are not with valorization, but with utilization and the continuation of social reproduction.

The post-labor role of human agency becomes apparent in the nature of the agency being automated: determinative judgment deskills the professional intelligent labor of experts, matching the Taylorist isolation and elimination of the intellectual dimensions of physical production. This replacement of social judgments with the fixed operation of a machine reiterates the process of transition from subsistence production to mass production: labor became dependent on industrial capitalism for all the material goods required for life in the nineteenth century; this deskilling of intellectual labor will create a comparable dependence on autonomous systems for those bureaucratic activities that have proliferated in response to the need for employment of experts. In transferring physical labor into new roles as intellectual labor, that work became increasingly routine and repetitive, proliferating out of a need to employ the workers who formerly occupied industrial positions. The expansion of leisure will produce similar expansive demands to occupy time and activity for the now-idled expert workers who no longer need to produce value but to occupy time. An expansion of demand for entertainment, spectacles, games, and arts is likely in the 'society of leisure.'

The deskilling of craft labor noted by critics of industrial manufacture in the nineteenth century—ranging from Karl Marx to art historian John Ruskin and the founder of the arts and crafts movement William Morris—led to a design reform movement that ultimately produced the reductive formalist arguments of Adolph Loos.[211] The difference posed by the deskilling of expertise necessitates a new, transformed role for human agency; what remains in this post-labor economy for human labor is the reflective judgment of creative synthesis, the analysis of questions for which there are neither fixed nor determinate answers—what philosopher Immanuel Kant identified as "genius," a creation that defies existing norms and expectations:

> [Genius is] something for which no determinate rule can be given, not a predisposition consisting of a skill for something that can be learned by following some rule or other.[212]

This elimination of human labor from routine and rote activities demonstrates the differential value given to those judgments that emerge from the application of rules, such as the mundane drudgery of industrial labor—versus those judgments that invent the rules themselves, such as the development of new production; this separation of reflection from determination is a restatement of René Descartes' "mind–body" duality.[213] This tension between labor and management becomes increasingly acute in industrial production, and exponentially more dramatic with the development of digital capitalism, suggesting an acceleration of class conflicts in the transition to a post-labor economy as the distinctions in the societal hierarchy break down. These social, political, and cultural differentials inhere in the heritage of Enlightenment thought that implicitly organizes capitalism and its valorization of human agency.

§ 6.3.1 Autonomous Management

Taylorism conceived of industrial human labor in machinic terms—unintelligent, fit only to perform those tasks set by the directive agency of management (design). This nihilistic force is emblematic of the operational priorities of digital capitalism that seek to maintain the status quo in spite of technological, environmental, and cultural change in the emergent post-labor economy that does not necessarily create a more just or humane workplace: the rote aspects of management can be automated as easily as the rote aspects of production. The fusion of pervasive monitoring in the workplace with the autonomous capacities of weak AI to responsively manage human labor creates an intrusive domination of precariat production[214] orchestrated through the use of automated overseers. It is a betrayal of the proffered emancipation of human labor by digital technology that creates an ever more authoritarian control over the productive process by strictly allocating only a limited quantity of time per task. This function of AI fuses its autonomy with the data collection of pervasive monitoring to create a mechanism that increases productivity by instrumentalizing the protocols of historical scientific management and then applying them to each worker individually, most clearly apparent in the *Amazon* warehouse where the manager of human labor—*the "packers"*—is a machine.[215]

This autonomous management of precariat labor depends on the compartmentalization and dislocation of production from any dimensions of both human intelligence and agency not required for the task at hand; this elision is a mechanism that diminishes the capacity for labor to resist or even challenge the implementation of AI through a complete regimentation of labor activity, yet this disenfranchisement is also a structural development in digital capitalism generally. The results of this technical control appear as economic productivity, but produce specifically domineering effects: the excessive workloads produced by an atomistic management of labor time leaves little other time to organize opposition. It is an attempt to force human labor to behave and perform in the role of a machine, with little concern for the physical, psychical, social and environmental costs of this mandated productivity. The parallels between the Amazon warehouse that has implemented this autonomous management and Sisyphean torture is obvious: a continually expanding task that can never be completed, yet is always demanding more labor. It provides a proximate index to the rapacity of on-demand distribution when matched with the contingent demands of incipient and expanding leisure.

§ 6.4 The Final Contradiction

AI reveals and exploits the differential between the material utility of commodities (need) and their social utility that stands entirely apart from their necessity in sustaining life (desire). These developments are especially apparent in how *Relational Art* in the 1990s made the social distinctions of class into the material of the work itself, a recognition that identifies how the 'society of leisure' challenges existing societal hierarchies. While economic factors are of primary importance to recognizing societal distinctions, they are secondary to the social inequalities they identify. This societal hierarchy arises as a product of how humans coordinate their social relationships through a complex of shifting, ambivalent, and contingent models of interaction-performance. Anthropologist Alan Fiske explains these behaviors through a limited set of four models that individuals employ to organize, understand, and plan their interactions with others. These applications are situational variables where relationships between individuals are not fixed, nor do they depend on routine to accommodate dynamic, novel interactions:

> Communal Sharing (CS) is a relationship in which people treat some dyad or group as equivalent and undifferentiated with respect to the social domain in question. [...] In Authority Ranking (AR) people have asymmetric positions in a linear hierarchy in which subordinates defer, respect, and (perhaps) obey, while superiors take precedence and take pastoral responsibility for subordinates. [...] AR relationships are based on perceptions of legitimate asymmetries, not coercive power; they are not inherently exploitative (although they may involve power or cause harm). [...] In Equality Matching [EM] relationships people keep track of the balance or difference among participants and know what would be required to restore balance. Common manifestations are turn-taking, one-person one-vote elections, equal share distributions, and vengeance based on an-eye-for-an-eye, a-tooth-for-a-tooth. [...] Market Pricing [MP] relationships are oriented to socially meaningful ratios or rates such as prices, wages, interest, rents, tithes, or cost-benefit analyses. Money need not be the medium, and MP relationships need not be selfish, competitive, maximizing, or materialistic—any of the four

> models may exhibit any of these features. MP relationships
> are not necessarily individualistic; a family may be the CS or
> AR unit running a business that operates in an MP mode
> with respect to other enterprises. [...] People often use
> different models for different aspects of their interaction
> with the same person.[216]

Social relationships are challenged by the problems of distribution created by automation: the post-labor economy disrupts wealth display models (AR) and (MP) that govern distribution, and displaces (EM) and (CS) through the proposition that no sharing is needed. AI intervenes in the use of these model interactions by creating anomalies in class position that subvert the societal hierarchy. Distinctions in consumption arise from differences in access to production (wealth), giving apparent separations of class or caste a correlation to the uneven and unequal distribution of commodities in quality, quantity, and type: rarer and more luxurious commodities are signs of greater wealth. These distinctions are symptom-effects of who receives a greater share of production, and the material nature of the share they receive—it is also a self-reinforcing mechanism that gives these class differences a durability in protecting social order and cohesion.

This differential distribution of production is the revenant heritage of pre-industrial Feudal society that has maintained a class system which denigrates both the poor and the unemployed as lazy, dirty, stupid, and uneducated. The Enlightenment challenge to Feudalism based in democratic discourse and debate does not eliminate these cultural separations in society, it accentuates them by emphasizing reflective judgment and dismissing the determinative judgments of production as a type of 'negative cognition' that does not involve creative thought, thus retaining the inherited distinctions of class. Social status displayed through the ability to waste commodities and labor defines class position,[217] a stratification that manifests itself as oppression—ageism, bigotry, chauvinism, exceptionalism, nationalism, racism, sexism, et. al.—and the assumption of criminality. This ideology depends on the reformation's mandate for moral uplift via labor as an argument "for perpetual effort and self-examination to the point of self-loathing"[218]—the intellectual labor of reflection for the upper echelons becomes physical labor for the lower classes. These views continue to shape the sociology of digital capitalism, posing cultural challenges to any attempt to mitigate technological unemployment and the impact of autonomous agency. The historical industrial system predicated upon a vast mobilization of human productive action directed into the creation and consumption of commodities that now finds itself rendered superfluous to that production with the proposition of a post-labor economy impedes the elimination of human labor because this hierarchy is the organization of cultural, political, and economic power.

Class based hierarchies are opposed by the egalitarian flattening of universal democracy.[219] When the wealthy engage in leisure they are not considered profligate criminals, yet the same cannot be said for the poor or middle classes. The same denigration of lower classes applies even more directly to unemployed and furloughed workers since they require public assistance to sustain themselves—their low social position allows them to be demonized as immoral, profligate, wastrels—being poor is the true crime for those at the top of the hierarchy, a teleological demonstration of inferiority. In emancipating labor from the necessity for productive action in a factory or other form of capitalist enterprise, this end to working must confront dual barriers to its emergence: the role of wealth in demonstrating the societal hierarchy, and the demonization of the handouts and other assistance historically granted to the poor when they are not in education, employment, or training. These incompatibilities proceed as expansions countered by containments that are simultaneously evident in/as the mass-production of commodities that undermines differences of social station, and affirmed by the dominance of management over labor in the factory. As *Pop* artist Andy Warhol noted, mass production instrumentalizes democratic and egalitarian proposals to eliminate societal hierarchies:

> You can be watching TV and see *Coca-Cola*, and you can
> know that the President drinks *Coke*, Liz Taylor drinks *Coke*,
> and just think, you can drink *Coke*, too. A *Coke* is a *Coke*, and
> no amount of money can get you a better *Coke* than the one
> the bum on the corner is drinking. All the *Cokes* are the same
> and all the *Cokes* are good. Liz Taylor knows it, the President
> knows it, the bum knows it, and you know it.[220]

The societal hierarchy serves to separate and isolate people into *a priori* groups that the democratic aspirations of mass production replace with a uniform understanding of people as equivalents or equals— the "mass" identified with the labor employed in the factory, rather than the elite management that directs that production. The industrial product is uniform, it converts all its consumers into the same mass: the "*Coke*" is equally available to everyone, identical and unchanging for different social strata. This egalitarian similarity of industrial production breaks down class differences when they are defined by differences in availability, access, or consumption of commodities; the 'society of leisure' accentuates this disruption. Cultural oppositions between the managerial order and that of democratic society is repeated by the organization of capitalist facture; acknowledging the similarity between social and economic organizations of society demonstrates their differences and the inherent structural conflict over how labor should be organized: either as isolated individuals whose authority to challenge the dictates of management are limited by the power differential, or as a group, such as a trade guild or union, that confront management as a "mass." The emergence of automation does not eliminate these power differentials, it simply displaces the "mass" of labor from being in a position to negotiate their role in production. AI does not undermine hieratic power, it magnifies it by enabling a fundamental displacement of labor from production.

The importance of excess, accumulation, and the display of wealth to the ideology of "autonomous achievement" are apparent in their role as social signifiers demonstrating relative positions within the established societal hierarchy; these ambivalent and ambiguous markers of social position become a determinate product of the instrumental operation of AI in architectural fantasies of control such as that proposed in *Sidewalk Lab's* urban redevelopment plan. Social and cultural roles under these social credit systems crystalize the existing hierarchy in a specific, fixed set of allowed activities that are then enforced by autonomous systems. Their "smart city" proposal in the 'yellow book' implements the control society described by Orwell's novel *1984* without apparent irony or self-awareness. By design it asserts a specific socio–cultural paradigm for how human society should operate as an extractive valorization for digital capitalism; as such it is a direct expression of this disrespect for individual autonomy and democratic processes that inheres in the Feudal order of the corporation. Ideology assumes a central role in the inclusion/exclusion dynamic instrumentalized in social credit by employing autonomous systems as gate keepers for access to either physical, immaterial, or informational "spaces." Social stratification is inherent in the event–productions of *Relational Art* that defy the creation of material commodities, but that nevertheless affirms the social distinctions apparent in the opposition between management and labor, as well as between surplus value (profit) and wages paid to labor. Social credit systems render the immaterial aspects of class distinctions as immanent rankings that formalizes those demonstrations of wealth made possible through the conspicuous "waste" of production, as Thorstein Veblen defines the term in *The Theory of the Leisure Class*:

> In the view of economic theory the expenditure in question
> is no more and no less legitimate than any other expenditure.
> It is here called "waste" because this expenditure does not
> serve human life or human well-being on the whole.[221]

The need to demonstrate social position, rather than merely service the requisite production to sustain physical life, is a metaphysical consumption of physical resources. This value is not merely indolence and caprice, but a conscious decision to demonstrate position through unnecessary expenditure. What were specifically cultural ways to identify different social positions become technological artifacts that maintain what were social distinctions in access and distribution. The identification of social status with wealth becomes increasing problematic as currency shifts to the right to demand production from being a marker for past production. This difference is increasingly marked by the affective role of production as a social practice, rather than being distinguished as a material commodity; these shifts are readily apparent in aesthetic tendencies, such as *Conceptual Art*, emergent alongside the digital computer in the 1960s, and growing still more prominent in the 1990s as digital technology reached a transition point between being a specialized office tool (word processing, spread sheets) and children's toy (video games) to being a omnipresent instrumentality for commerce, communication, and social activity.[222] These discursive impacts of digital technology become apparent in the ways that it borrows from aesthetic concepts as much as it influences them.[223] The emergent dominance of immaterial facture comes along side the emergence of social relationships into being the subject of aesthetic production, a contradictory development that illuminates both emergences as the opposed sides of this final contradiction—the role of production in establishing and maintaining societal hierarchies, as Nicolas Bourriaud describes for *Relational Art*:

> [1990's] art thus prompts us to envisage the relations between space and time in a different way. Essentially, moreover, it derives its main originality from the way this issue is handled. What, actually, is *concretely produced* by artists such as Liam Gillick, Dominique Gonzales-Foerster and Vanessa Beecroft? What, in the final analysis, is the object of their work? [224]

All these artists that Bourriaud identifies are known for their creation of art/event-spectacles where afterwards no 'art object' remains as such: documentary photographs and news coverage describe what happened, but there is no remnant object in the way that even *Conceptual Art* left behind *things* that can be collected, exhibited, and examined as aesthetic production. The *Relational Art* in these examples lies in the commodification of sociality created by the spectacle of the exhibition, a factor especially apparent in the relational works by Rirkrit Tiravanija. The social function that separates the audience for these works from the general public becomes their "substance"—and this social relationship is the commodity being exchanged. It is a liquidation of the substance of artwork, replaced by a commodification of the class distinction: *who* was at the art/event becomes significant, rather than the commodity-object itself. There is nothing, (or almost nothing) physical to collect. The "labor" of the artist is directly converted into the art in a development whose origins in *Conceptual Art* are readily apparent. The work cannot be resold, auctioned off, or directly collected, yet it does not escape commodification, merely undermine the capacity to be collected as a precious artifact or fetish object. Instead, the value of this art lies in the social status apparent in the "bragging rights" offered by having been in attendance at these art/event spectacles. *Relational Art's* aesthetics are a literalization of the social dynamics Guy Debord noted in *The Society of the Spectacle* unironically becoming the productive mechanism of art itself:

> The spectacle is the self-portrait of power in the age of
> power's totalitarian rule over the conditions of existence.[225]

The affective and social functions reified in contemporary art via the creation of an exclusive and exclusionary experience affirms Veblen's identification of the ability to "waste" resources as having a social function, as being a class marker. The prominence of *Relational Art* is not a direct response to digital automation, but a symptom of the cultural change underway, recognizable in the utopian propositions of the Internet and digital facture common in the 1990s.

Elevation to the "leisure class" potentially offered by the displacement of human labor by AI depends on the distribution of titles to future production; the capacity to demand facture that inheres in the established hierarchies of economic, cultural and social power is a function of a structural organization that is neither egalitarian nor democratic, and which works to conserve the status quo organization of the social. AI is a structural challenge: not merely to the organization or production of commodities, but because of the contradiction between wages::profits, it also challenges the distribution of its products as well. The issue of who benefits from the automation of agency is a question that cannot be only answered by the owners of the technology.

Replacing labor with automous agency expands the productive role for agnotology::surveillance as a deterrent of the structural changes the post-labor economy necessarily begins: AI masks this imbalance by proposing pervasive monitoring as a mechanism for control, complemented by the role of agnotology in managing dissent through a dissolution of consensus into irrational factions, each with "their own facts." The individuation of social agency this process creates is both a reflection of the uniquely identified consumer and the need to dissolve social relationships to prevent opposition—two forms of control that depend on the synthesis of data accomplished by AI systems that enable mass identification through surveillance, such as facial recognition.

These factors contain the social displacements by offering them as an individual (personal) hardship rather than as structural operations whose only solution lies with the problem of distribution.

§ 6.4.1 The Automation of Societal Position

The "Social Credit System" formally implemented in China, (and proposed as a part of the "smart city" being developed by *Sidewalk Labs*), gamifies the societal hierarchy as an AI system in an attempt to convert the fluid and dynamic social interaction–performance in society into a quantified judgment of class position. This instrumentalized system of pervasive monitoring tracks citizens and automates their punishment for violating its prescriptions on individual behavior. It converts Fiske's (AR) and (MP) models that describe these hieratic differences in society by differentiating who has rights to which production into a predetermined set of privileges enforced by automated punishments. The implementation of social credit transforms these internalized guides employed by members of society into a technology that reifies social endeavor as instrumentality, converting metastable social interaction into a fixed network of *a priori* privileges and permissions. It is a system of ubiquitous control whose authoritarian nature attempts to assure its perpetual dominance by substituting itself for cultural and social relationships—the Chinese state not only teaches and arbitrates behavior, but assumes a legislative role over the cultural and social order via autonomous pronouncements that are unquestionable. The constant monitoring and punishment fashioned by social credit is an intrusive, gamified authoritarianism only possible because of AI. In becoming an instrumentality rather than a social construction— especially in the form of credential verification and identification— digital automation instrumentalizes social distinctions, making opposition and challenge to them much more difficult. The same fusion of social control and AI systems features prominently in the development plan for a "smart corporate-owned city" that implements continuous pervasive monitoring in an architectural 'space' in the proposal by *Sidewalk Labs* called the 'yellow book':

> The 437-page book documents how much private control of city services and city life *Google* parent company *Alphabet Inc.'s* leadership envisioned when it created the company, which could soon be entitled to some of the most valuable underdeveloped real estate in North America, estimated by one firm to be worth more than half-a-billion dollars.[226]

The proposal for this real estate development by *Sidewalk Labs* makes its extensive use of pervasive monitoring and social credit essential to the provision of social services and the allocation of resources within this "city." The 'yellow book' proposal describes a fully-privatizedsociety run without democratic oversight; there are no public resources in this proposal, even though they are financed through taxation. This privately-owned "public space" modeled on the Lake Buena Vista suburb attached to the *Walt Disney World* theme park in Florida requires residents to 'share information' or else receive a restricted level of social services; this development is a non-governmental version of the same social credit schema being deployed for totalitarian control in China, achieved by replacing governmental oversight with corporate control:

> *Sidewalk* will require tax and financing authority to finance and provide services, including the ability to impose, capture, and reinvest property taxes.[227]

The 'yellow book' proposal makes the implicit element of social control without democratic accountability an unavoidable consequence of constructing this system. Combined with the coercive demand that residents surrender their autonomy to receive social services from the corporation assuming governmental duties—and paid for through taxation on residents—creates an explicitly technological analogue to the Feudal control over social resources and their allocation. This consolidation of a dominant authority supported by a transfer of power from democratically accountable government to profit-driven private corporation enables the transfer of the cultural authority of social relationships and interactions to autonomous systems.

The invention and implementation of social credit is not merely an invasion of privacy, nor is it a dystopian fantasy; it derives from the structural priorities that lead to the invention of machine learning and autonomous agency: the denigration and rejection of any intelligent labor apart from that of the highest levels of capitalist production. It shows the anti-democratic foundations of these disparate authoritarian orders and makes the conflict between the mass of labor inevitable since etymologically 'demos' means the commoners, the crowd, rather than the elites. Understanding the cultural conflict between post-labor and its proposition of the 'society of leisure' then becomes coherent in immediately obvious terms: it is the opposition between the minority who control the machines through their ownership, and the rest of society that has become dependent on these devices for their survival. It accentuates the dependency on machine production that began with the industrial revolution.

§ 6.5 The Problem Posed for Universal Basic Income

Universal basic income (UBI) or "basic income" is a uniform distribution of currency to citizens living in a specific society without restraint or restriction on what they may do with the money. It appears as a solution to the structural imbalances revealed in/by autonomous agency in that it offers a resolution to the problem of distribution without requiring any changes to the productive organization of society. As such, UBI implies a potential continuation of the *status quo* hierarchy without creating the need for radical alterations in the allocation of existing wealth or addressing the structural inequalities inherent in the ideology of "autonomous achievement." A universal basic income offers a corrective for the structural imbalance created by automation and its displacement of labor from the circulation of wages::profits necessary to maintain capitalist production as it is currently organized. However, any variant of UBI will likely receive significant opposition in countries such as the United States, that are ideologically predisposed to reject the UBI system as a "hand out" or "entitlement program" that cannot be paid for without increasing taxation. The trinity of cultural impedimenta to its adoption derive from the ways that social class combined with capitalist production as the societal hierarchy: [a] the religious prohibitions on idleness; [b] the role of wealth in social status display; [c] the "Protestant Work Ethic" that ties lower class identity to their role in labor ("honest hard work"). Fiscal barriers to UBI are simply problems of monetary policy; the issue that AI creates for society is a problem or *spending* rather than *monetarism*—factors that the 'great decoupling' makes self-evident. Because the elimination of human labor is an enforced and necessary idleness for these societies, the 'underclass' displaced by AI are "not worth troubling about"[228]—what has historically been associated with the leisure classes is activity linked to wealth, cultural prestige, and a dominant social position; it is commonly denied to those classes who perform the human labor of production.

The implementation of UBI has a potential to solve the obsolescence of human labor, if and only if the full elimination of human work is the goal; restrictions on who receives UBI are attempts to retain the *status quo* social order with its structural regulation of access to *production–distribution–consumption* and the societal hierarchy it maintains. As a solution to structural change and technological unemployment, this development is not a utopian proposal of an end to scarcity and the triumph of humanist or Enlightenment values, although the implementation of autonomous agency is their apex and an expression of their conclusive goal. Nevertheless, the revolution of AI and automation will produce social upheaval and societal dislocation no matter what solutions to its challenges are adopted. Digital automation renders redundant and irrelevant a large segment of humanity whose labor is no longer required, desired, or necessary. For any society that equates an individual's significance to their value as labor, this replacement by machinery is catastrophic. UBI only appears to be an economic solution because it adapts the existing mechanisms of commodity distribution—access to production mediated by individual wealth—without changing existing economic processes. The distribution and restriction of access to commodities by wealth can continue unabated by the 'society of leisure' because the degrees of leisure available within the societal hierarchy remain unchanged. The result of using UBI to maintain the *status quo* without a recognition that AI involves a fundamental shift in the nature and quantity of human agency required in production is obvious: it will not address the emergent social, political, and economic challenges posed by digital automation. If UBI is used to sustain a desperate, destitute, and unjust distribution of production the crisis created by autonomous agency will not end—it is a cultural conflict between democratic order and a revenant Feudal order enshrined as the capitalist business enterprise, apparent in the consolidation of corporate power. This crisis is an ideological failing, reified economically: the cultural dominance of "autonomous achievement" implemented as the societal hierarchy created by capitalism depends on the distinction between the work performed by management and that performed by labor—when AI eliminates human labor from determinative judgment it makes the work performed by labor and management converge.

The discrepancy between a just, equitable, and democratic society, and the structural imbalances of capitalist acquisition, wealth hoarding, and conspicuous consumption are neither easily resolved, nor are privileges of any kind ever willingly surrendered. To produce a just society depends on the equitable distribution of commodities—the surplus values generated by these autonomous machines must be redistributed to society as a whole in the same way that wages transform surplus value in a continuous cycle mediated by governmental expenditures and taxation. Using AI in an attempt to resolve concerns with the rate of profit is a chimera that imagines capitalism as something other than a zero-sum relationship. The titles to production distributed by UBI must represent the majority of surplus values created by digital automation otherwise the extractive role of autonomous production will create a scarcity of capital; to allow UBI to serve the fantasy of wages as lost profits enables a concentration of wealth unseen outside Feudal societies where the "king" owns everything and what the subjects receive depends entirely on their capricious sense of *noblesse oblige*. Achieving either the just or unjust society once AI dismisses labor from production requires a radical reordering of the priorities of capitalism, one that involves the recognition that our social organization is dependent on labor to keep order by occupying the majority of people's time with paid activities that enable (are essential to) their survival. The idleness of unemployment differs from the inactivity of leisure only through the distinction of social status; in both cases no productive actions are being performed—their separation is a cultural value rather than an essential difference.

The society of leisure assumes an expansion of democratic plurality that UBI appears to provide; this egalitarian outcome is an illusion. The lesson of disruptive technologies is that their ability to force change decreases with time as they approach dominance; as AI becomes dominant, the changes it effects in society with become increasingly difficult to alter, and the social adaptations to its displacements will assume the appearance of inevitable teleological results of the structural demands imposed by maintaining the *status quo*. This cultural barrier is the true impediment to the 'society of leisure' and the stability of a post-labor economy. The "creative destruction" produced by technological change results in a powerful counter-action, as Schumpeter explains:

> The opening up of new markets, foreign or domestic, and the organizational development from the craft shop and factory to such concerns as *U.S. Steel* illustrate the same process of industrial mutation—if I may use that biological term—that incessantly revolutionizes the economic structure *from within*, incessantly destroying the old one, incessantly creating a new one. This process of Creative Destruction is the essential fact about capitalism.[229]

The instability that Schumpeter terms "creative destruction" produces a metaphoric Brownian motion for society—a continuous churn and change—within what is a structurally fixed range. Film director Martin Scorsese's objections to "franchise pictures" are a critical comment on his industry's attempts to address the crisis for cinema created by new markets and technology. These factors of disruption and instability are inherent to the capitalist marketplace because the innovations of industrial capitalism depend on technological and sociological changes that each require cultural adaptation. Their impacts begin as economic turmoil: new inventions pose new problems for existing companies competing within the same marketplace. The proposition of UBI has a specific function for these dynamics as a social mitigation that *mutatis mutandis* maintains this *status quo* by enabling the retirement of human labor by replacing the wages in the cycle of wages::profits, thereby supporting the continuation of value circulation that Schumpeter describes; however, this replacement creates an extractive concentration of wealth that creates its own pathologies. This continuous motion of currency that enables the continuation of production is also its precondition for existence: precisely the cyclic relationships of *production–distribution–consumption* that digital production and automation undermine.

The shift to "leisure" and obsolescence of human-generated value that AI and digital automation makes possible is not something that capitalism is ideologically equipped to understand, address, or accept: *not working* is and has been conceived as immoral, prodigal, profligate, so the displacements and idleness imposed on human labor by digital automation will likely be enormously destructive to social order. Nevertheless, the post-labor transition is fundamentally ambivalent: it might produce either a society of greater injustice and inequality, magnifying the problems of the present, or could create a society that is more just and equal. Choices about commodity distribution and the structural continuity with *status quo* hierarchies and consumption will determine the eventual outcome. As a society, we are still at the very early stages of this shift. The familiar capitalist problems of determining the ideal allocation of labor and resources to maximize profit generation does not match the new problems posed by automation, resource depletion, environmental degradation, and an aging population neither able to work, nor necessary for the production of value. What outcome we choose depends on the models we have for understanding our current situation—as our received and historical models are in the process of falling away and do not provide answers for the new potentials of digital capitalism and the social configuration emerging in response to machine learning and autonomous agency. These existing models are products of older, established beliefs, assumptions, and ideology developed in response to a different configuration of *production–distribution–consumption*; to develop a critique of these changed conditions requires a changed model. However, old inequalities and oppressions do not disappear simply because a new revolution offers a potential for a better future free from the authoritarian excesses and abuses of the past. Freedom requires maintenance; justice is not a given. To achieve such an outcome, the conditions of possibility must first be recognized, and the structural demands that impede such a development need to be fully appreciated for the inertia they represent. We are at the inception of the post-labor economy, a moment before the 'society of leisure' emerges, and all the fantasies and the terrors of *what might be* form impediments to any clear appraisal of *what is.*   Ω

AFTERWORD

This much is obvious:

AI is an automaton that serves the demands of its human owners.

Still, questions proliferate: *Who are these owners and will they always be the same group? What will be the nature of their demands? Will they use 'social credit' to control society? Will AI only respond to those demands or also work to produce them through subtle manipulations?* Answers for the cultural problems posed by autonomous agency lie in the future, but its invention will produce a disruptive reorganization of human society that is already underway with the 'great decoupling.'

This book started with the foundational question: *What exactly does AI automate?* My answer began with 'agency,' the same concept that was a central philosophical concern of the Enlightenment. While it may be tempting to claim the transferal of human agency to an autonomous machine as proposed by AI pioneer John McCarthy would mean that this apparatus achieves a closure for the Enlightenment project by making human agency into an instrumentality, the arrival of this conclusion may still be premature. The automated systems and autonomous agency of contemporary AI that displaces labor from production does not need to use language, form abstractions, or devise concepts to operate. Instead of being a terminus to the Enlightenment and its influence, it could just as easily be its democratic flowering as the demand for a general emancipation of humanity from the restrictive drudgery of fixed roles arrives as the 'society of leisure'—but that outcome is as likely to be a fantasy as the dystopian emergence of a "robot overlord." The digital computer performs complex operations via machine learning that enables it to match the cognitive labor of human intelligence when confronting questions with fixed outcomes that follow what are determinate organizations of information. Most production, whether skilled or unskilled, physical or intellectual, is a rote application of fixed knowledge systems that only produces a limited quantity of outcomes, making most human labor entirely subject to automation by either weak or strong AI systems.

Everything else is a fantasy that belongs to the realm of Parnassus, the domain of oracles, seers, and the unknown. Societies are dynamic, unstable churns of cultural tendencies meeting and opposing structural demands that are in constant transformation, making any attempt to explain the future quite absurd: prognostications on the future are always a vision of the present moment when they are pronounced, a dressed up exaggeration masquerading as novelty, visionary imagination, and socio–cultural manifesto in equal degrees. The proposition of the 'society of leisure' is a hypothetical outcome, yet to be determined, and its articulation was *not* the purpose of this study. The utility of digital capitalism as a model for both the familiar uses of weak AI and the potential applications of strong AI lies with its capacity to predict issues in the as-yet unknown social, cultural, and political dimensions of a post-labor economy. This capacity to anticipate, to identify trends, or to provoke discussion by raising issues about *how* to consider the new development of autonomous agency produced by the invention of machine learning was the purpose of this discursive approach to cultural questions raised by this technology.

Critical analysis can serve as a diagnostic for these cultural developments, helping to shape the future while it seeks to describe the present: this discursive questioning of the transformation of human agency into the automation of refractive and determinative judgments is an attempt to understand how AI challenges the status quo, rather than being a declaration of jubilee and immanent utopia. The model of digital capitalism offered by this examination is neither meant as a nihilistic assessment of the present, nor as a dystopian proposal of the future, but as an identification of currently active tendencies.

The structural contradictions between capitalism and the 'society of leisure' this analysis considered are cultural hurdles that block the deployment of AI as an emancipatory force, limiting the social capacity to adapt to the changes it promises to create by restricting its benefits to a reification of the status quo, because those who have privileges rarely surrender them willingly, seeking to affirm and maintain their power and position for themselves and their descendants in ways that make surrendering their benefits from the existing societal hierarchy unlikely. Instead, the rigid instrumentalities of AI and digital systems generally encourage an inflexibility in thought apparent in the ideological purity informed by scanning words and actions for the least flicker of impurity, offense, immorality which then must be punished more strenuously for being subtle and almost undetectable. This cultural enforcement is "social credit," and it encourages an internalizing of the panopticon of pervasive monitoring, promoting the impassive, inscrutable mask described by George Orwell as a defense against the authoritarian in his novel *1984*.

Any technology that elevates the lower classes in a cultural hierarchy creates the same impact as a lowering those classes located at the top, since it is precisely this matter of distance between the top and bottom that is important to a caste system. The issue is exactly the distance, the ability of those at the top to stand over those at the bottom, that makes the emergence of an free, egalitarian, democratic social order fundamentally challenging—it always confronts the accumulation of prestige and position as an insurrectionary force that over time makes *de facto* divisions in society into *de jure* protections that maintain the established order against challenges. The perception that these privileges are being threatened provides a powerful tool to demagogues seeking power, their erosion or replacement with an order that involves the elimination of privilege can only promote greater social upheaval. The ideological mechanisms that express social differences—the various biases and prejudices: ageism, bigotry, chauvinism, exceptionalism, nationalism, racism, sexism, et. al.—are difficult to eliminate since their cultural function is precisely an assertion of a dominant position, to announce and maintain class difference and privilege; they become more pronounced as a response to the elimination of these differences. Upheavals of social order often end in revolutions, counter-revolutions, reigns of terror, and catastrophic wars: the past does not die willingly that the future may be born.   Ω

December, 2019

REFERENCES

NOTES TO PREFACE

1   Muro, M.; Whiton, J.; Maxim, R. *What Jobs are Affected by AI? Better-Paid, Better-Educated Workers Face the Most Exposure* (Washington: Brookings Institute, 2019), pp. 5-6.

2   Holland, J. *Hidden Order: How Adaptation Builds Complexity* (Reading: Perseus Books, 1995) p. 79.

3   Acemoglu, D. and Restrepo, P. "Automation and New Tasks. How Technology Displaces and Reinstates Labor" *Journal of Economic Perspectives* vol. 33, no. 2 (Spring 2019) pp. 3-30. doi: 10.1257/jep.33.2.3

4   Frey, C.B.; Osborne, M.A. "The Future of Employment: How Susceptible are Jobs to Computerization?" *Technological Forecasting and Social Change,* vol. 114 (January 2017) pp. 254-280. doi: 10.1016/j.techfore.2016.08.019

5   Schumpeter, J. *Capitalism, Socialism, and Democracy* (New York: Harper Perennial, 2008) p. 188.

6   Lears, T. J. J. *No Place of Grace: Anti-Modernism and the Transformation of American Culture 1880-1920* (New York: Pantheon, 1981) pp. 19-20.

7   Schumpeter, J. *Capitalism, Socialism, and Democracy* (New York: Harper Perennial, 2008) p. 173.

8   Acemoglu, D. and Restrepo, P. "Automation and New Tasks: How Technology Displaces and Reinstates Labor" *Journal of Economic Perspectives* vol. 33, no. 2 (Spring 2019) pp. 3-4.

9   Acemoglu, D. and Restrepo, P. "Automation and New Tasks. How Technology Displaces and Reinstates Labor" *Journal of Economic Perspectives* vol. 33, no. 2 (Spring 2019) pp. 3-30. doi: 10.1257/jep.33.2.3

[10] Bastani, A. *Fully Automated Luxury Communism* (New York: Verso, 2019).

[11] Veblen, T. *The Theory of the Leisure Class* (New York: Dover, 1994) p. 9.

[12] Kant, I. "Section 1: Pure Reason in its Dogmatic Use" *The Critique of Pure Reason* trans. Werner Pluhar (Indianapolis: Hackett Publishing Company, 1987) p. 675.

[13] Cherry, F. "Idle Hands Are The Devil's Workshop" *Bible Reasons* https://biblereasons.com/idle-hands-are-the-devils-workshop/ posted January 2, 2019; accessed December 15, 2019.

[14] Crawford, K.; Dobbe, R.; Dryer, T.; Fried, G.; Green, B.; Kaziunas, E.; Kak, A.; Mathur, V.; McElroy, E.; Sánchez, A.N.; Raji, D.; Rankin, J.L.; Richardson, R.; Schultz, J.; West, S.M.; Whittaker, M. *AI Now 2019 Report* (New York: AI Now Institute, 2019) pp. 49-52.

[15] Poggioli, R. *The Theory of the Avant-garde,* (Cambridge: Harvard University Press, 1968) p. 137.

[16] Werner, R. "Can Banks Individually Create Money Out of Nothing?—The Theories and The Empirical Evidence" *International Review of Financial Analysis* vol. 36 (December 2014) pp. 1-19. doi: 10.1016/j.irfa.2014.07.015

[17] Veblen, T. *The Theory of the Leisure Class* (New York: Dover, 1994) pp. 18-19.

[18] Abbing, H. *Why are Artists Poor? The Exceptional Economy of the Arts,* (Amsterdam; Amsterdam University Press, 2004) p. 307.

[19] Johnson, C.B. *Modernity Without A Project* (Brooklyn: New York, 2014) pp. 42-53.

[20] Morris, R. "Thoughts on *Hegel's Owl* (2002)" *Have I Reasons: Work and Writings 1993–2007* edited by Nena Tsouti-Schillinger (Durham: Duke University Press, 2008) p. 163.

[21] Schumpeter, J. *Capitalism, Socialism, and Democracy* (New York: Harper Perennial, 2008) p. 188.

NOTES TO § 1.

[22] Betancourt, M. *The Critique of Digital Capitalism* (Brooklyn: Punctum Books, 2016) p. 186.

[23] Schumpeter, J. *Capitalism, Socialism, and Democracy* (New York: Harper Perennial, 2008) pp. 31-32.

[24] Schumpeter, J. *Capitalism, Socialism, and Democracy* (New York: Harper Perennial, 2008) p. 79.

25 Kant, I. "Section 1: Pure Reason in its Dogmatic Use" *The Critique of Pure Reason* trans. Werner Pluhar (Indianapolis: Hackett Publishing Company, 1996) p. 675.

26 Gillick, L. "The Good of Work" *Are You Working Too Much? Post-Fordism, Precarity, and the Labor of Art* (Berlin: Sternberg Press, 2011) p. 70.

27 Schumpeter, J. *Capitalism, Socialism, and Democracy* (New York: Harper Perennial, 2008) p. 87.

28 Levy, F. and Murnane, R.J. *The New Division of Labor: How Computers are Creating the Next Job Market* (Princeton: Princeton University Press, 2004) pp. 19-21.

29 Crawford, K.; Dobbe, R.; Dryer, T.; Fried, G.; Green, B.; Kaziunas, E.; Kak, A.; Mathur, V.; McElroy, E.; Sánchez, A.N.; Raji, D.; Rankin, J.L.; Richardson, R.; Schultz, J.; West, S.M.; Whittaker, M. *AI Now 2019 Report* (New York: AI Now Institute, 2019) pp. 49-50.

30 Schumpeter, J. *Capitalism, Socialism, and Democracy* (New York: Harper Perennial, 2008) p. 83.

31 LeWitt, S. "Sentences on Conceptual Art" *Concept Art*, ed. Ursula Meyer, (New York: Dutton, 1972) pp. 174-175.

32 Obermeyer, Z.; Powers, B.; Vogeli, B.; Mullainathan, S. "Dissecting Racial Bias in an Algorithm Used to Manage the Health of Populations" *Science* vol. 366, issue 6464 (2019) p. 447-448. doi: 10.1126/science.aax2342

33 Kolozova, K. *Towards a Radical Metaphysics of Socialism* (New York: Punctum Books, 2015) p. 66.

34 Warsh, D. *Knowledge and the Wealth of Nations* (New York: Norton, 2006).

35 Taylor, F. *The Principles of Scientific Management* (New York: Harper, 1911) p. 39.

36 Ashby, W. *Introduction to Cybernetics* (London: Chapman & Hall, 1957) p. 9.

37 Fleming, M.; Clarke, W.; Das, S.; Phongthiengtham, P.; Reddy, P. "The Future of Work: How New Technologies Are Transforming Tasks" *MIT-Watson AI Lab* (October 31, 2019) https://mitibmwatsonailab.mit.edu/research/publications/paper/download/The-Future-of-Work-How-New-Technologies-Are-Transforming-Tasks.pdf accessed December 1, 2019.

38 Kant, I. "IV. On Judgment as a Power that Legislates A Priori" *The Critique of Judgment*, trans. Werner Pluhar (Indianapolis: Hackett Publishing Company, 1987) p. 19.

39   Ngai, S. *Out Aesthetic Categories: Zany, Cute, Interesting* (Cambridge: Harvard University Press, 2012) pp. 117-121.

40   Holland, J. *Hidden Order: How Adaptation Builds Complexity* (Reading: Perseus Books, 1995) p. 34.

41   Attali, J. *Noise: The Political Economy of Music* (Minneapolis: University of Minnesota Press, 1985) p. 6.

42   Bohm, D. *Wholeness and the Implicate Order* (New York: Routledge, 1980) p. 5.

43   Kant, I. "Transcendental Judgment in General" *The Critique of Pure Reason,* trans. Werner Pluhar (Indianapolis: Hackett Publishing Company, 1996) pp. 206-209.

44   Bohm, D. *Wholeness and the Implicate Order* (New York: Routledge, 1980) p. 6.

45   Bohm, D. *Wholeness and the Implicate Order* (New York: Routledge, 1980) p. 16

46   Barthes, R. *The Responsibility of Forms* (Berkeley: The University of California Press, 1985) p. 137.

47   Garrison, M. "The Poetics of Ambivalence" *Archetypal Psychiatry* (Spring 1982) pp. 226-227.

48   Garrison, M. "The Poetics of Ambivalence" *Archetypal Psychiatry* (Spring 1982) p. 227.

49   Betancourt, M. *Ideologies of the Real in Title Sequences, Motion Graphics and Cinema* (New York: Routledge, 2019) pp. 73-78.

50   Bleuler, E. *Dementia Praecox, or the Group of Schizophrenias* (New York: International Universities Press, 1950) pp. 271-286.

51   Garrison, M. "The Poetics of Ambivalence" *Archetypal Psychiatry* (Spring 1982) pp. 226-230.

52   Bleuler, E. "Theory of Schizophrenic Negativism" translated by William A. White, *Journal of Nervous and Mental Disease* (1950) p. 266.

53   Betancourt, M. "Technesthesia and Synaesthesia" *Harmonia: Glitch, Movies and Visual Music* (Cabin John: Wildside Press, 2018) pp. 145-148.

54   These are the images included in the book *Anth(r)optic* by Ethan Ham & Benjamin Rosembaum, (Oakland: The Present Group, 2007).

55   Mordvintsev, A.; Olah, C.; Tyka, M. "Inceptionism: Going Deeper into Neural Networks" *Google AI Blog* https://ai.googleblog.com/2015/06/inceptionism-going-deeper-into-neural.html posted June 17, 2015; accessed December 13, 2019.

56   Dalí, S. *Oui* (Boston: Exact Change, 1998) p. 180.

57   Breton, A. *Manifestos of Surrealism* (Ann Arbor: The University of Michigan Press) p. 26.

58   Saussure, F. *Course in General Linguistics* trans. Roy Harris (Chicago: Open Court Classics, 1986) pp. 65-98.

59   Eco, U. *A Theory of Semiotics* (Bloomington: Indiana University Press, 1979) pp. 40-47.

60   Garrison, M. "The Poetics of Ambivalence" *Archetypal Psychiatry* (Spring 1982) pp. 228-230.

61   Barthes, R. *The Responsibility of Forms* (Berkeley: The University of California Press, 1985) p. 141.

62   Chomsky, N. *Syntactic Structures* (The Hague/Paris: Mouton, 1957) p. 15.

63   Pennycook, G.; Rand, D.G. "Lazy, not biased: Susceptibility to partisan fake news is better explained by lack of reasoning than by motivated reasoning" *Cognition* no. 188 (July, 2019) pp. 39-50. doi: 10.1016/j.cognition.2018.06.011

64   Martin, K. "Marcel Duchamp's *Anémic Cinéma*" *Studio International* vol. 189, no. 973 (January-February 1975) p. 54.

65   Jakobson, R. "On the Verbal Art of William Blake and other Poet-Painters" *Linguistic Inquiry* vol. 1, no. 1 (January, 1970) pp. 3-23.

66   Gray, C. "The Great Spectator" interview *Art in America* vol. 57, no. 4 (July-August, 1969) p. 21.

67   Cabanne, P. *Dialogues with Marcel Duchamp* trans. Ron Padget (New York: Viking, 1971) p. 43.

68   Sitney, P. A. *Modernist Montage,* (New York: Columbia University Press, 1990) p. 25.

69   Martin, K. "Marcel Duchamp's *Anémic Cinéma*" *Studio International* vol. 189, no. 973 (January-February 1975) pp. 53-60.

70   Vassilakis, N. "The Last Vispo: *toward vispoetics*" *The Last Vispo Anthology: Visual Poetry, 1998–2008* ed. Craig Hill and Nico Vassilakis (Seattle: Fantagraphics Books, 2008) pp. 8-10.

71   Kant, I. "IV. On Judgment as a Power that Legislates A Priori" *The Critique of Judgment* trans. Werner Pluhar (Indianapolis: Hackett Publishing Company, 1987) pp. 19-20.

72   Kant, I. "IV. On Judgment as a Power that Legislates A Priori" *The Critique of Judgment* trans. Werner Pluhar (Indianapolis: Hackett Publishing Company, 1987) pp. 19-20.

[73] Veblen, T. *The Theory of the Leisure Class* (New York: Dover, 1994) p. 24.

[74] The animated film *Last Days of Coney Island* (2015) by Ralph Bakshi was produced independently of both studio financing (via crowd funding) and production staff by using digital technology.

[75] The Adobe software *AfterEffects* allows a real time puppeting of animated characters using a video camera for motion tracking/capture and AI to map a face to that animation.

NOTES TO § 2.

[76] Deleuze, G. and Guattari, F. *The Anti-Oedipus: Capitalism and Schizophrenia* (Minneapolis: University of Minnesota Press, 1983) pp. 222-234.

[77] Marx, K. *Capital: Volume 1* (London: Penguin Classics Reprint edition: 1990) p. 5.

[78] Marx, K. *Capital: Volume 1* (London: Penguin Classics Reprint edition: 1990) p. 154.

[79] Skidelsky, R. *Money and Government: The Past and Future of Economics* (New Haven: Yale University Press, 2019).

[80] LeWitt, S. "Sentences on Conceptual Art" *Concept Art* ed. Ursula Meyer (New York: Dutton, 1972) pp. 174-175.

[81] LeWitt, S. "Sentences on Conceptual Art" *Concept Art* ed. Ursula Meyer (New York: Dutton, 1972) pp. 174-175.

[82] Weiner, L. 1968 and 1970 statements reproduced in *Six Years: The Dematerialization of the Art Object* ed. Lucy Lippard (Berkeley: University of California Press, 1997) pp. 73-74.

[83] Lippard, L. *Six Years: The Dematerialization of the Art Object from 1966 to 1972* (Berkeley: University of California Press, 1997) p. 42.

[84] Calinescu, M. *The Five Faces of Modernity (Revised Edition)* (Durham: Duke, 1987).

[85] Kant, I. "§14 Elucidation by Examples" *The Critique of Judgment* trans. Werner Pluhar (Indianapolis: Hackett Publishing Company, 1987) p. 71.

[86] Rand, A. *Atlas Shrugged* (New York: Penguin Group, 2005) p. 140.

[87] Schumpeter, J. *Capitalism, Socialism, and Democracy* (New York: Harper Perennial, 2008) p. 188.

[88] That this belief in an unfettered marketplace is a juvenile fantasy is so obvious as to not merit mentioning.

[89] Marx, K. *Grundrisse (The Fragment on Machines)* (London: Penguin Classics, 1993) p. 692.

[90] Preston, S. "Reputations Made and in the Making" *The New York Times* (18 April, 1965) np.

[91] Goodman, C. *Digital Visions: Computers and Art* (New York: Abrams, 1987).

[92] Lippard, L. *Six Years: The Dematerialization of the Art Object from 1966 to 1972* (Berkeley: University of California Press, 1997) p. 25.

[93] Noll, A. M. "Computers and the Visual Arts" *Design and Planning 2: Computers in Design and Communication* ed. Martin Krampen and Peter Seitz (New York: Hastings House, 1967) pp. 65-79.

[94] Popper, F. *Art of the Electronic Age* (New York: Abrams, 1993) pp. 78-80.

[95] Levy, S. *Hackers: Heroes of the Computer Revolution* (New York: Penguin, 1994) pp. 39-49.

NOTES TO § 3.

[96] Marx, K. *Capital: Volume 1* (London: Penguin Classics Reprint edition: 1990) p. 92.

[97] Marx, K. *Capital: Volume 1* (London: Penguin Classics Reprint edition: 1990) p. 9.

[98] Kramer, A.; Guillory, J.; Hancock, J. "Experimental Evidence of Massive-Scale Emotional Contagion Through Social Networks" *Proceedings of the National Academy of Sciences* issue 24 (June 17, 2014) 111:8788–8790.
doi: 10.1073/pnas.1320040111

[99] Noll, A.M. *Highway of Dreams: A Critical View Along the Information Superhighway* (New York: Routledge Digital Editions, 2010) p. 89.

[100] Marx, K. *Capital: Volume 1* (London: Penguin Classics Reprint edition: 1990) pp. 8-9.

[101] Marx, K. *Capital: Volume 1* (London: Penguin Classics Reprint edition: 1990) p. 154.

[102] Deleuze, G. "Postscript on the Societies of Control" *October* vol. 59 (Winter, 1992) pp. 3-7.

[103] Delaney, K. "The Robot That Takes Your Job Should Pay Taxes, Says Bill Gates" *Quartz* https://qz.com/911968/bill-gates-the-robot-that-takes-your-job-should-pay-taxes/ posted February 17, 2017; accessed December 6, 2019.

[104] Veblen, T. *The Theory of the Leisure Class* (New York: Dover, 1994) p. 29.

[105] Scorsese, M. "I Said Marvel Movies Aren't Cinema. Let Me Explain." *The New York Times* (November 4, 2019). https://www.nytimes.com/2019/11/04/opinion/martin-scorsese-marvel.html

[106] Scorsese, M. "I Said Marvel Movies Aren't Cinema. Let Me Explain." *The New York Times* (November 4, 2019). https://www.nytimes.com/2019/11/04/opinion/martin-scorsese-marvel.html

[107] Baumol, W.J. and Bowen, W.G. *Performing Arts: The Economic Dilemma, a study of problems common to theater, opera, music and dance* (New York: The Twentieth Century Fund, 1966) pp. 172-180.

[108] Owens, C. "The Discourse of Others: Feminists and Post-Modernism" *The Anti-Aesthetic* ed. Hal Foster (Seattle: The Bay Press, 1983) p. 57.

[109] Owens, C. "The Discourse of Others: Feminists and Post-Modernism" *The Anti-Aesthetic* ed. Hal Foster (Seattle: The Bay Press, 1983) p. 57.

[110] Farris, P.W.; Bendle, N.T.; Pfeifer, P.E.; Reibstein, D.J. *Marketing Metrics: The Definitive Guide to Measuring Marketing Performance* (Upper Saddle River: Pearson Education, 2010).

[111] Baumol, W.J. and Bowen, W.G. *Performing Arts: The Economic Dilemma, a study of problems common to theater, opera, music and dance* (New York: The Twentieth Century Fund, 1966) p. 164.

[112] Helland, E. and Tabarrok, A. *Why Are the Prices so Damn High?* (Arlington: The Mercatus Center, 2019) pp. 36-37.

[113] Shaviro, S. *Post Cinematic Affect* (Washington: Zero Books, 2010) pp. 132-133.

[114] Gaudreault, A and Marion, P. *Kinematic Turn: Film in the Digital Era and Its Ten Problems* trans. Timothy Barnard (Montreal: Caboose Books, 2012) p. 40.

[115] Buden, B. "Criticism Without Crisis: Crisis Without Criticism" *Art and Contemporary Critical Practice: Reinventing Institutional Critique* ed. Gerald Raunig and Gene Ray (London: May Fly, 2009) pp. 33-42.

[116] Hagener, M., Hediger V. and Strohmaier, A. *The State of Post-Cinema* (London: Palgrave, 2016) p. 3.

[117] Arnheim, R. *To The Rescue of Art: Twenty-Six Essays* (Berkeley: University of California Press, 1992) p. 36.

[118] Maltby, R. "A Brief Romantic Interlude: Dick and Jane go to 3 1/2 Seconds of the Classical Hollywood Cinema" *Post-Theory: Reconstructing Film Studies* ed. David Bordwell and Noel Carroll (Madison: University of Wisconsin Press, 1996) p. 435.

[119] Greenberg, C. "Modernist Painting" *Clement Greenberg: The Collected Essays and Criticism, Volume 4* ed. John O'Brian (Chicago: University of Chicago Press, 1993) p. 86.

[120] Hatfield, J. "Expanded Cinema and Narrative" *Millennium Film Journal* nos. 39–40 (Winter 2003) pp. 63–64.

[121] Partch, H. *Genesis of a Music* (Madison: University of Wisconsin Press, 1949).

[122] Poggioli, R. *The Theory of the Avant-Garde* (Cambridge: Harvard University Press, 1968) p. 56.

[123] Danto, A. *After the End of Art* (Princeton: Princeton, 1997) p. 45.

[124] Basualdo, C. "A Writing Without Literature (or Painting as a Construction Site)" *Painting Zero Degree* (New York: Independent Curators, 2000) pp. 10-16.

[125] Owens, C. "The Discourse of Others: Feminists and Post-Modernism" *The Anti-Aesthetic* ed. Hal Foster (Seattle: The Bay Press, 1983) p. 57.

[126] Gillick, L. "The Good of Work" *Are You Working Too Much? Post-Fordism, Precarity, and the Labor of Art* ed. Julieta Ardanda, Brian Kuan Wood, and Anton Vidokle (Berlin: Sternberg Press, 2011) pp. 70-72.

NOTES TO § 4.

[127] Lears, T.J. Jackson. *No Place of Grace: Anti-Modernism and the Transformation of American Culture, 1880-1920* (New York: Pantheon, 1981) pp. 19-20.

[128] Betancourt, M. "Article: a107, Disruptive Technology: The Avant–Gardness of Avant–Garde Art" *CTheory* (May 1, 2002) np.

[129] Arendt, H. *Eichmann in Jerusalem: A Report on the Banality of Evil* (New York: Viking Press, 1963) p. 248.

[130] "Freight Facts and Figures" *US Department of Transportation, Bureau of Transportation Statistics* https://datahub.transportation.gov/stories/s/45xw-qksz accessed Dec 8, 2019.

[131] Webb, M. "The Impact of Artificial Intelligence on the Labor Market" *Stanford University* https://web.stanford.edu/~mww/webb_jmp.pdf posted November 2019; accessed December 17, 2019.

132 Kumar, D. "Rural America is Losing Young People—Consequences and Solutions" *Wharton Public Policy Initiative, The University of Pennsylvania* https://publicpolicy.wharton.upenn.edu/live/news/2393-rural-america-is-losing-young-people- posted March 23, 2018 accessed December 7, 2019.

133 Agnotology maintains the stability of exchange values by impeding their rational evaluation by obstructing price discovery. This obfuscation is an essential feature of how agnotological acts to debase rationality, leaving only affective and personal beliefs as a rationale for decision making.

134 Betancourt, M. *The Critique of Digital Capitalism* (Brooklyn: Punctum Books, 2016) pp. 215-224.

135 Rarick, C. "Confucius on Management: Understanding Chinese Cultural Values and Managerial Practices" *Journal of International Management Studies* vol. 2, no. 2 (August 2007) pp. 22-28. http://www.jimsjournal.org/3%20Charles.pdf

136 Schumpeter, J. *Capitalism, Socialism, and Democracy* (New York: Harper Perennial, 2008) p. 188.

137 Standing, G. *The Precariat: The New Dangerous Class* (London: Bloomsbury Academic, 2016).

138 Foglesong, R. "Planning the Capitalist City" *Readings in Planning Theory, Second Edition* ed. Scott Campbell and Susan S. Fainstein (London: Blackwell, 2003) p. 105.

139 Foglesong, R. "Planning the Capitalist City" *Readings in Planning Theory, Second Edition* ed. Scott Campbell and Susan S. Fainstein (London: Blackwell, 2003) p. 103.

140 Veblen, T. *The Theory of the Leisure Class* (New York: Dover, 1994) pp. 24-29.

141 Katyal, S. "Semiotic Disobedience" *Washington University Law Review,* vol. 84., no. 2 (2006) p. 493.

142 May, C.; Sell, S. K. *Intellectual Property Rights: A Critical History* (Boulder: Lynne Rienner Publishers, 2005) p. 5.

143 Katyal, S. "Semiotic Disobedience" *Washington University Law Review,* vol. 84, no. 2 (2006) p. 493.

144 "Understand YouTube Rights Management — YouTube Help," *Google.com* https://support.google.com/youtube/answer/4597810?hl=en accessed November 13, 2019.

145 Katyal, S. "Semiotic Disobedience" *Washington University Law Review,* vol. 84, no. 2 (2006) p. 549.

[146] Danto, A. *Beyond the Brillo Box* (Berkeley: University of California Press, 1990) p. 191.

[147] "Understand YouTube Rights Management — YouTube Help," *Google.com* https://support.google.com/youtube/answer/4597810?hl=en accessed November 13, 2019.

[148] "What is an Asset? — YouTube Help," *Google.com* nd; accessed November 13, 2019 https://support.google.com/youtube/answer/4597810?hl=en

[149] Jones, A. "New York Dada: Beyond the Readymade" *The Dada Seminars* ed. Leah Dickerman with Matthew S. Witkovsky (New York: Distributed Art Publisher, 2005) pp.151-172.

[150] Loos, A. "Ornament and Crime" *Crime and Ornament: The Arts and Popular Culture in the Shadow of Adolf Loos* ed. Bernie Miller and Melony Ward (New York: XYZ Books, 2002) pp. 29-36.

[151] Veblen, T. *The Theory of the Leisure Class* (New York: Dover, 1994) p. 60.

[152] Edwards, R. "The Art of Work" *"The Art that is Life": The Arts & Crafts Movement in America, 1875-1920* ed. Wendy Kaplan (Boston: Bulfinch Press, 1987) pp. 233-235.

[153] Shahn, B. *The Shape of Content* (New York: Vintage, 1957) p. 67.

[154] *American Canvas* (Washington: National Endowment for the Arts, 1997).

[155] O'Doherty, B. *Inside the White Cube* (Berkeley: University of California Press, 1999).

[156] Brenson, M. *Visionaries and Outcasts* (New York: The New Press, 2001).

[157] Fry, R. "The French Post-Impressionists (preface to catalog for the Second Post-Impressionist exhibition, 1912)" *Vision and Design* (London: Pelican Books, 1937) pp. 195-196.

[158] Williams, C. *Realism and the Cinema: A Reader* (London: Routledge, 1980) p. 11.

[159] Dalrymple Henderson, L. "Mysticism, Romanticism, and the Fourth Dimension" *The Spiritual in Art: Abstract Painting 1890–1985* (New York: Abbeville Press, 1986) pp. 219-238.

[160] Rand, P. *Thoughts on Design* (New York: Van Norstrand Reinhold, 1970) p. 9.

[161] Rickey, G. *Constructivism (Revised Edition)* (New York: George Braziller, 1995).

[162] Barker, Tim. "Aesthetics of the Error: Media Art, the Machine, the Unforseen, and the Errant" *Error: Glitch Noise and Jam in New Media Cultures* ed. Mark Nunes (New York: Bloomsbury, 2011) pp. 46-48.

[163] Allport, G. W. *The Nature of Prejudice* (New York: Perseus, 1954).

NOTES TO § 5.

[164] Schwartz , B. *The Paradox of Choice: Why More Is Less, Revised Edition* (New York: Ecco Press, 2016).

[165] Bleuler, E. *Dementia Praecox, or the Group of Schizophrenias* (New York: International Universities Press, 1950) p. 91.

[166] Bleuler, E. *Dementia Praecox, or the Group of Schizophrenias* (New York: International Universities Press, 1950) p. 266.

[167] Bleuler, E. *Dementia Praecox, or the Group of Schizophrenias* (New York: International Universities Press, 1950) p. p. 271-286.

[168] Halle, H. *The Personal is Political*, sculpture, 1992.

[169] Hutson, J.; Taft, J.; Barocas, S.; Levy, K. "Debiasing Desire: Addressing Bias & Discrimination on Intimate Platforms" *Proceedings of the ACM on Human-Computer Interaction* vol. 2, no. CSCW, article 73 (November 2018). doi: 10.1145/3274342

[170] Notopoulos, K. "The Dating App That Knows You Secretly Aren't Into Guys From Other Races" *Buzzfeed News*https://www.buzzfeednews.com/article/katienotopoulos/coffee-meets-bagel-racial-preferences posted January 14, 2016; accessed December 10, 2019.

[171] Gelles, D. "Inside Match.com: It's all about the algorithm" *Slate* https://slate.com/human-interest/2011/07/inside-match-com-it-s-all-about-the-algorithm.html posted July 30, 2011; accessed December 10, 2019.

[172] Koppel, N. and Ovide, S. "EHarmony Settles Dispute Over Gay Matches" *The Wall Street Journal* https://www.wsj.com/articles/SB122714242388642779 posted November 20, 2008; accessed December 10, 2019.

[173] Taylor, V. "Eugenics Is Influencing Dating Apps and Other Forms of Tech" We Are Your Voice https://wearyourvoicemag.com/sex-and-health/eugenics-dating-apps-tech-science posted December 10, 2019; accessed December 10, 2019.

[174] Orwell, G. *1984* (New York: Houghton Mifflin Co., 1977) p. 3.

175 In the United States, the legal protections to digital information on cellphones granted in 2014 in *Riley vs. California* create privacy protections against police intrusions, it does not address the myriad exploits of digital technology, nor does it consider the use of EULA agreements by corporations to consecrate their use of surveillance as a condition of ownership and use of hardware or software.

176 Krebs, B. "The *iPhone 11 Pro's* Location Data Puzzler" *Krebs on Security* https://krebsonsecurity.com/2019/12/the-iphone-11-pros-location-data-puzzler/ posted December 3, 2019 accessed December 5, 2019.

177 Betancourt, M. *The Critique of Digital Capitalism* (Brooklyn: Punctum Books, 2016) pp. 191-214.

178 "Wilf Hey" *Free Online Dictionary of Computing* http://foldoc.org/%2bWilf%2bHey accessed December 18, 2019.

179 Jensen, R. "The Myth of the Neutral Professional" *Questioning Library Neutrality: Essays from Progressive Librarian* ed. Alison Lewis. (Duluth: Library Juice Press, 2008) pp. 89-96.

180 Sap, M.; Card, D.; Gabriel, S.; Choi, Y.; Smith, N.A. "The Risk of Racial Bias in Hate Speech Detection" *Proceedings of the 57th Annual Meeting of the Association for Computational Linguistics, Florence, Italy, July 28-August 2, 2019* (Florence: Association for Computational Linguistics, 2019) pp. 1668–1678.

181 Kim, P. "Data-Driven Discrimination at Work" *William & Mary Law Review* vol. 48 (2017) pp. 857–936.
doi: https://ssrn.com/abstract=2801251.

182 Obermeyer, Z.; Powers, B.; Vogeli, B.; Mullainathan, S. "Dissecting Racial Bias in an Algorithm Used to Manage the Health of Populations" *Science* vol. 366, issue 6464 (2019) p. 453.
doi: 10.1126/science.aax2342

183 Jensen, R. "The Myth of the Neutral Professional" *Questioning Library Neutrality: Essays from Progressive Librarian* ed. Alison Lewis (Duluth: Library Juice Press, 2008) pp. 89-96.

184 Obermeyer, Z.; Powers, B.; Vogeli, B.; Mullainathan, S. "Dissecting Racial Bias in an Algorithm Used to Manage the Health of Populations" *Science* vol. 366, issue 6464 (2019) pp. 447–453.
doi: 10.1126/science.aax2342

185 Angwin, J.; Larson, J.; Mattu, S.; Kirchner, L. "Machine Bias," *ProPublica*, (May 23, 2016) https://www.propublica.org/article/machine-bias-risk-assessments-in-criminal-sentencing

[186]   Obermeyer, Z.; Powers, B.; Vogeli, B.; Mullainathan, S. "Dissecting Racial Bias in an Algorithm Used to Manage the Health of Populations" *Science* vol. 366, issue 6464 (2019) p. 453. doi: 10.1126/science.aax2342

[187]   Pally, M. *Sex and Sensibility: Reflections on Forbidden Mirrors* (New York: Ecco Press, 1994).

[188]   Office of the Mayor, "Mayor de Blasio Signs Executive Order to Establish Algorithms Management and Policy Officer," *The Official Website of the City of New York* (November 19, 2019) https://www1.nyc.gov/office-of-the-mayor/news/554-19/mayor-de-blasio-signs-executive-order-establish-algorithms-management-policy-officer

[189]   Schumpeter, J. *Capitalism, Socialism, and Democracy* (New York: Harper Perennial, 2008) pp. 84-88.

[190]   Crawford, K.; Dobbe, R.; Dryer, T.; Fried, G.; Green, B.; Kaziunas, E.; Kak, A.; Mathur, V.; McElroy, E.; Sánchez, A.N.; Raji, D.; Rankin, J.L.; Richardson, R.; Schultz, J.; West, S.M.; Whittaker, M. *AI Now 2019 Report* (New York: AI Now Institute, 2019) pp. 49-52. https://ainowinstitute.org/AI_Now_2019_Report.html

[191]   Wagner, K. "Facebook Sets Goal to Double Female Workforce in Five Years" *Bloomberg.com* https://www.bloomberg.com/news/articles/2019-07-09/facebook-sets-goal-to-double-female-workforce-in-five-years posted July 9, 2019; accessed November 26, 2019.

[192]   Veblen, T. *The Theory of the Leisure Class* (New York: Dover, 1994) p. 24.

[193]   LeWitt, S. "Sentences on Conceptual Art" *Concept Art* ed. Ursula Meyer (New York: Dutton, 1972) pp. 174-175.

[194]   West, J.; Grind, K.; McMillan, R.; Schechner, S. "How Google Interferes With Its Search Algorithms and Changes Your Results" *The Wall Street Journal* https://www.wsj.com/articles/how-google-interferes-with-its-search-algorithms-and-changes-your-results-11573823753 November 15, 2019.

[195]   Brewster, T. "Google Hands Feds 1,500 Phone Locations In Unprecedented '*Geofence*' Search" *Forbes.com* https://www.forbes.com/sites/thomasbrewster/2019/12/11/google-gives-feds-1500-leads-to-arsonist-smartphones-in-unprecedented-geofence-search/#5ebb942327dc posted December 11, 2019; accessed December 12, 2019.

[196]   "Google Search consumer information" *Google Search Help* https://support.google.com/websearch/answer/7585859?hl=en accessed November 29, 2019.

[197] Speri, A. "The NYPD Kept an Illegal Database of Juvenile Fingerprints for Years" *The Intercept* (November 13, 2019) https://theintercept.com/2019/11/13/nypd-juvenile-illegal-fingerprint-database/

[198] Scorsese, M. "I Said Marvel Movies Aren't Cinema. Let Me Explain." *The New York Times* (November 4, 2019). https://www.nytimes.com/2019/11/04/opinion/martin-scorsese-marvel.html

[199] Communications Decency Act of 1996, 47 U.S.C. § 230 June 19, 1934, ch. 652, title II, §230, as added Pub. L. 104-1041996; amended Pub. L. 105-2771998; Pub. L. 115-164 Apr. 11, 2018, 132 Stat. 1254 (1996).

[200] Angwin, J.; Grassegger, H. "Facebook's Secret Censorship Rules Protect White Men From Hate Speech But Not Black Children" *ProPublica* https://www.propublica.org/article/facebook-hate-speech-censorship-internal-documents-algorithms posted June 28, 2017; accessed December 10, 2019.

NOTES TO § 6.

[201] Federici, S. *Caliban and the Witch* (Brooklyn: Autonomedia, 2004) pp. 21-60.

[202] Freeberg, E. *The Age of Edison: Electric Light and the Invention of Modern America* (New York: Penguin, 2014).

[203] Muro, M.; Whiton, J.; Maxim, R. *What Jobs are Affected by AI? Better-Paid, Better-Educated Workers Face the Most Exposure* (Washington: Brookings Institute, 2019) p. 11.

[204] Eco, U. *The Limits of Interpretation* (Bloomington: Indiana University Press, 1994) p. 83.

[205] Johnson, C.B. *Modernity Without A Project* (Brooklyn: Punctum Books, 2014) pp. 59-60.

[206] McLeay, M.; Radia, A.; Thomas, R. "Money Creation in the Modern Economy" *The Bank of England Quarterly Bulletin* Q1 (2014) pp. 14-28.

[207] Werner, R. "Can Banks Individually Create Money Out of Nothing?—The Theories and The Empirical Evidence" *International Review of Financial Analysis* vol. 36 (December 2014) pp. 1-19 doi: 10.1016/j.irfa.2014.07.015.

[208] Morgan, R. C. *The End of the Art World* (New York: Allworth Press, 1998), p. 67.

[209] Poggioli, R. *The Theory of the Avant-Garde* (Cambridge: Harvard University Press, 1968) pp. 17-40.

[210] Foglesong, R. "Planning the Capitalist City" *Readings in Planning Theory, Second Edition* ed. Scott Campbell and Susan S. Fainstein (London: Blackwell, 2003) p. 103.

[211] Pevsner, N. *Pioneers of Modern Design* (Bath: Palazzo, 2004) pp. 13-34.

[212] Kant, I. "§46 Fine Art is The Art of Genius" *The Critique of Judgment* trans. Werner Pluhar (Indianapolis: Hackett Publishing Company, 1987) p. 175.

[213] Descartes, R. *Meditations on First Philosophy: with Selections from the Objections and Replies* ed. John Cottingham (Cambridge: Cambridge University Press, 1996).

[214] Standing, G. *The Precariat: The New Dangerous Class* (New York: Bloomsbury USA, 2011).

[215] Knight, W. "Inside Amazon's Warehouse, Human-Robot Symbiosis" *MIT Technology Review* https://www.technologyreview.com/s/538601/inside-amazons-warehouse-human-robot-symbiosis/ posted July 7, 2015; accessed 12 December, 2019.

[216] Fiske, A. P. "Human Sociality" http://www.sscnet.ucla.edu/anthro/faculty/fiske/relmodov.htm accessed 22 November 2019.

[217] Veblen, T. *The Theory of the Leisure Class* (New York: Dover, 1994) p. 60.

[218] Journalist Barbara Ehrenreich quoted discussing her book *Smile or Die* in a book review. Murray, J. "*Smile or Die: How Positive Thinking Fooled America and the World* by Barbara Ehrenreich" *The Observer* https://www.theguardian.com/books/2010/jan/10/smile-or-die-barbara-ehrenreich posted January 10, 2010; accessed December 3, 2019.

[219] Gilens, M. and Page, B.I. "Testing Theories of American Politics: Elites, Interest Groups, and Average Citizens" *Perspectives on Politics* vol. 12, no. 3 (September, 2014) doi: 10.1017/S1537592714001595 p. 566.

[220] Warhol, A. *The Philosophy of Andy Warhol* (San Diego: Harvest, 1977) pp. 100-101.

[221] Veblen, T. *The Theory of the Leisure Class* (New York: Dover, 1994) p. 60.

[222] Schiller, D. *Digital Capitalism: Networking the Global Market System* (New Haven: The MIT Press, 1999).

[223] Bourriaud, N. *Relational Aesthetics* trans. Simon Pleasance and Fronza Woods (Dijon-Quetigny: Les Presses du Reel, 2004) pp. 66-71.

[224] Bourriaud, N. *Relational Aesthetics* trans. Simon Pleasance and Fronza Woods (Dijon-Quetigny: Les Presses du Reel, 2004) pp. 48.

[225] Debord, G. *The Society of the Spectacle* trans. Donald Nicholson-Smith (New York: Zone Books, 1994) p. 19.

[226] Cardoso, T. and O'Kane, J. "Sidewalk Labs document reveals company's early vision for data collection, tax powers, criminal justice" *The Globe and Mail* https://www.theglobeandmail.com/business/article-sidewalk-labs-document-reveals-companys-early-plans-for-data/ posted October 30, 2019; accessed November 27, 2019.

[227] Cardoso, T. and O'Kane, J. "Sidewalk Labs document reveals company's early vision for data collection, tax powers, criminal justice" *The Globe and Mail* https://www.theglobeandmail.com/business/article-sidewalk-labs-document-reveals-companys-early-plans-for-data/ posted October 30, 2019; accessed November 27, 2019.

[228] Schumpeter, J. *Capitalism, Socialism, and Democracy* (New York: Harper Perennial, 2008) p. 188.

[229] Schumpeter, J. *Capitalism, Socialism, and Democracy* (New York: Harper Perennial, 2008) p. 83.

CPSIA information can be obtained
at www.ICGtesting.com
Printed in the USA
LVHW030709221121
704087LV00001B/111

9 781479 448197